LLANELLI
From a Village to a Town
by
Geoffrey N. Morgans

An environmentally friendly book printed and bound in England by
www.printondemand-worldwide.com

Mixed Sources
Product group from well-managed
forests, and other controlled sources
www.fsc.org Cert no. TT-COC-002641
© 1996 Forest Stewardship Council
FSC

PEFC Certified
This product is
from sustainably
managed forests
and controlled
sources
www.pefc.org
PEFC
PEFC/16-33-415

This book is made entirely of chain-of-custody materials

LLANELLI: FROM A VILLAGE TO A TOWN

Copyright © Geoffrey N Morgans 2015

A catalogue record for this book is available from the British Library

ISBN 978-178456-239-7

First published 2015 by Mike Clarke Printing

An imprint of Upfront Publishing of
Peterborough, England.

LLANELLI
From a Village to a Town
by
Geoffrey N. Morgans

CHAPTERS

The origins of Llanelly lie within the Roman colonisation of South Wales, and appears to have been a simple encampment between Loughor to the east, which was an established fort, and their progress to Carmarthen which was a terminus for the two routes taken to this station.

The northerly route, from Brecon through Llandovery to Carmarthen over the mountains, whilst the southerly route covered Caerleon, Neath, Lougher and Carmarthen via Llanelly along the Bury estuary.

Kidwelly has a much longer history than Llanelly. The environs of Kidwelly Castle were built by William de Londres in 1084, and the Castle in 1106, although destroyed by Llewellyn The Great in 1230 the Castle was rebuilt in 1270. Throughout the Middle Ages Kidwelly was one of the most important townships in South Wales, as a consequence Llanelly was administered under the medieval system as a commot (subordinate) by the cartref of Kidwelly. The borough of Kidwelly was further enhanced by the granting of a number of charters between 1113 and 1444, when an incorporation as a Chartered Borough was granted by King Henry VI. The Charter was subsequently reaffirmed in 1541 and 1551. In 1619 James I granted a further Charter under which the Borough of Kidwelly was administered until 1885, when the Borough was incorporated under the local authority. The 800 year old corporation was dissolved and with it the rights, powers and authorities ceased.

Throughout this period, Llanelly, under this administration developed from a hamlet of some twelve households in 1556 to a township of 2972 inhabitants in Llanellys first census of 1801. The oldest building in Llanelly is its Parish Church on the site of which a church has existed since the 6th century, although none of the present structure relates to earlier than the 12th century and in that only the tower can be attributed to that period; and later a pillar bearing the date 1683 during possible renovations.

The structure of the main body of the church was renovated in 1823 and 1845, and prior to this a small schoolroom was added adjoining the tower in 1806. The church takes its name from Saint Elle, a patron saint who was the daughter of Brychan Bryncheiniog a sixth century Welsh chieftain and a cousin of Saint David the patron saint of Wales. The town takes its name from the Parish Church, Llan being the english translation of the Welsh "Church" hence Llanelly, the church of Elly.

Church records prior to 1754 are fragmented, often dependent upon the literacy of the incumbent, but at that time the law on regulation changed and the calendar adopted the new style of marriages solemnised within the church, from which records are unbroken.

The original design of the church included a second tower of spire design two thirds of the way along the roof behind the main tower. This rare feature was only one of the very few to be built in Britain, the purpose of which was thought to house a Sanctus Bell which was rung during mass at the elevation of the host. The significance of the spine is now academic as it was demolished in the renovations of 1823.

By 1845, due to the standard of workmanship of the earlier renovation in the main, the church was again in dire need of refurbishment, in particular the roof which was in a state of serious dilapidation that it leaked badly. Encumbent on this restoration was the intention to increase the seating capacity of the church. Some facets of the church were again lost on the "restorers" as in the process the ancient south porch was demolished, main oak beams removed and the old three deck pulpit taken away. They did however achieve some of their objectives, with the outer walls raised and new windows fitted, and the erection of a new gallery at the west end capable of seating some one hundred and fifty worshippers. The church was re-opened after seven months by the Lord Bishop of St. Davids, and the tower with its six bells made in 1828 by J. Kingston a founder of Bridgewater lived on. In 1854 the organ was erected, and all remained intact until 1906, when it was again deemed necessary to effect major repairs. This was to be the most radical change to the structure of all; whilst the tower itself was restored with little change to its image, the rest of the church was rebuilt from its foundations.

A basement chamber was excavated under the north chancel aisle to accommodate heating, and the high ground outside to the north face excavated to a depth of a foot below the inner floor level to some seven feet away from the foundations to prevent the ingress of surface water. To further enhance the dryness and heat retention, the inner walls were relined.

The external walls were rebuilt for the most part of stone salvaged from the original structure and reset in the manner of the old tower. The roof was rebuilt using slate, and the original south porch and bell turret reconstructed in the form originally designed; thus the church was returned in outward appearance to that resembling the structure as it would have been in the 15th century.

The internal work was mainly of renovation and redecoration. The organ was restored and two octaves of pedal pipes added, the ancient font was redressed and reset to its original position near the entrance, coats of arms and tablets having been cleaned were redistributed throughout the church. Finally the old memorial slabs were relaid in the west porch and organ chamber, all of the work was carried out without altering the original cruciform plan lying east to west as the structure was rebuilt on the original foundations.

The church has some interesting vessels in its keep, one of which that is still in use is a silver chalice inscribed "Poculum Eclesie de Llanelly" dated 1574 which was presented to the church by Queen Elizabeth Ist.

The church clock which dates back to around the mid 1700's was converted to run from electric power in 1968 where previously it was hand wound once every day.

On a lighter note, it is reported that the tower was on more than one occasion used by the town's Fire Brigade, around 1912, to test their catching sheets for people trapped in tall buildings. A member of the Brigade would leap off the 70 foot tower to be caught by his colleagues in the sheet, there is no record of insurance covering this dangerous practice.

Commercial coal mining has existed in the Llanelly area since early 1550 when exporting of coal was recorded. However it was not until domestic demand increased in the 18th century that it reached a peak, and although growth was halted in 1829 during the industrial recession it did recover to carry through to the 20th century.

Many of the earliest mine workings were simple drift mines as deep mining to depths of more than 1200 ft. did not appear until 1850. These early workings were spread over a wide area and tapped the more than twenty seam stratum running mainly east to west across the area. The small private and individually owned workings used antiquated methods and consequently the early miners suffered greatly under poor working and safety conditions. Many, some as young as six years of age, died in catastrophic accidents or were maimed for life over these years, although no figures are available on this account as none were published.

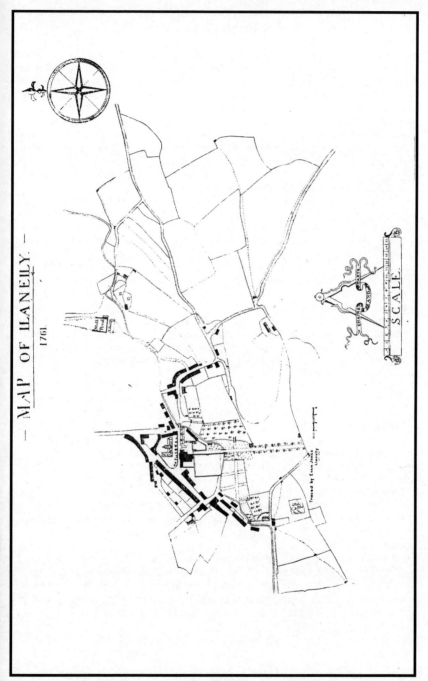

- MAP OF LLANELLY -

1761

SCALE.

Traced by Evan Jones
Llanelly

CHAPTER TWO
THE BIRTH OF INDUSTRY

Following the years of depression expansion was very limited until 1750, after which industrialists from outside the area encouraged by the evolution of technology took an interest in the Llanelly coalfields. Development in the years between 1750 and 1795 were hesitant until a second wave of outside industrialists moved in to supplement the efforts of the then local entrepreneurs. This was occasioned by the greater use of coal in other industries, one of the earliest being the erection of an iron furnace and foundry in the Furnace area of the town, the interests of which passed to Alexander Raby in 1796. His interest served to exploit the rich veins of coal reserves under the lands of the local landowners, in particular those of the Mansell family who owned the Stradey Estates.

Alexander Raby, both wealthy and of some stature, committed all his effects and capital into his industrial interests in Llanelly and at the same time took a keen interest in local affairs and those of his employees to whom he was known as a decent employer who paid a good wage. Unfortunately following the depression the furnace was blown out in 1815 and the forge declined until it finally closed in 1820. Most of his fortune by then had practically gone and he retired to Wells in Somerset where he died at the age of 88 in 1835. His wife Ann predeceased Raby and died in Llanelly in 1824 aged 78 and was buried in the Parish Church.

Alexander Raby's son, Arthur Raby, relinquished the families interests due to the accumulation of debts to all other than coal mining, of which he held grants at Caereithin and colliery shipping leases. He continued to attempt to expand these to no avail and was effectively taken over by Neville and Druce to avoid bankruptcy in 1926.

Over the thirty odd years from 1800, many other notable English industrialists in the example of Raby arrived on the scene with varying interests, this to some extent had an adverse effect on the local population in that the local landowners gave up their interests in the locality, and the influx of skilled foreigners eroded the language and traditional outlook of the locals.

In 1800 South Wales produced around 90% of Britains' copper, mostly in the area between Neath and Swansea where many smelting works had become established. Charles Neville became the manager of a copperworks in Swansea in 1795, but inadequate supplies and price variations in the supply of coal caused him to consider relocation. The site finally chosen was at Llanelly, and in 1805 the Llanelly Copperworks Co. was formed by Messrs. Daniel & Co. at the rear of the Copperworks Road site of the present Company.

To ensure tenure of supply, the Copperworks Co., became involved in coal mining in 1807 which further involved interest in the rail and shipping of coal. The interest in the docks was enhanced in that it allowed the copper ore to be shipped in and coal to be exported by return journeys, a practice which was to become a major function of the business strategy of the Company.

When in February 1816, Neville purchased the Rabys, collieries it further immursed the Company in the mining industry as it also gave them control of the Stradey Estates collieries. Many other acquisitions followed, including those of General Ward, and the Copperworks Co. emerged as the largest single concern to operate in the Llanelly coalfield, whilst the Nevilles were recognised as the leading 19th century industrialists in the area during their years in control.

Prior to 1750 the coal mined in Llanelly was transported from source using animals fitted either with panniers or drawing carts to the various shipping points, bearing in mind that demand was low at that time and driven mainly by its export trade. As the volumes increased to 1830, many small canals and tramways were constructed to transfer the coal to the shipping places, so that almost every colliery or group of mining interests had its own transportation system.

Ultimately the volume became such that this system too was inadequate and the need for more efficient handling brought about the railway system as the preferred method of transportation. Steam locomotive power became established nationally in 1840, and the South Wales main line railway opened through Llanelly in 1852.

This brought to the fore the importance of the shipping places to the coal trade as the docking areas along the Bury estuary were tidal and in itself subject to major silting at its various inlets. The problem was further compounded by the fact that the mineworkings were being further developed inland. This had effect on almost every dock in the estuary as Carmarthen Dock, Pembroke Dock, Llangennech Quay, Dafen Pill and Townsend Pill were all tidal, only the new dock at Machynys Pool and Copperworks Docks were floating docks. Such was the physical and geological nature of the Bury estuary that shipping was a hazardous occupation, borne out by the many shipping fatalities over the years, which severely hindered the coal trade by this method, and this has been the main reason why Llanelly was never developed as a seaport even through the twentieth century.

A divergence to the metal and coal industries came about in the shape of the establishment of a pottery in the town. The founder of the pottery was one William Chambers Jnr., a member of a locally well known family with industrial and landowning interests in the area. His father, William Chambers Snr. Built the pottery for a sum reported to have been £10,000, and the family at that time resided in Llanelly House opposite the Parish Church in Bridge Street.

Many of the original skilled workers in Llanelly came from the Glamorgan Pottery at Swansea which closed down in 1839, others came from as far afield as Stoke on Trent. The Chambers owned the pottery until 1858 apart from a short lease to Coombs and Holland through financial difficulties between 1855 and 1858 when it returned to Chambers. Shortly after the release a new lease to Holland who with a later partner David Guest continued its operation until 1875. It closed again after that but reopened again in 1877, this time under the direction of David Guest and his cousin Richard Dewsbury. The pottery finally closed down in 1923.

The main products produced in the early years were table services and toilet seats, and a limited number of hand painted breakfast sets, vases and mugs.

The latter often with a rose or fruit decoration, but each one individual in its design. Around 1878 it was acknowledged that the South Wales Pottery at Llanelly was the only manufacturer of "Blue on White" earthenware in Wales.

Of the famous names associated with Llanelly Pottery, Samuel Walter Shufflebotham stands head and shoulders above all others. Born in Leek in Staffordshire in 1876, he moved to Bristol in 1908 where he married. Shortly after he moved to Llanelly to take up employment in the Llanelly Pottery where he remained until 1915 at which time he returned to Bristol for a short period before retiring to Torquay.

Shufflebothams influence on the design and hand painting of Llanelly Pottery was immense, and examples of his fine work in the style of Bristol and Wemyss are the most sought after examples of Llanelly ware.

Another of the notables employed at the Pottery was Sarah Jane Roberts who produced most of the Cockerel ware. Generally this design is found on plates and bowls although a small number did appear on mugs. In all cases the cockerel was painted to face to the left, the reason for which is unknown, the design however was thought to be based upon a much earlier French pottery design.

The Pottery had strong links with Park Street Chapel and later Park Congregational Church which are identified later; but it is often noted that some plates bore the names of Capel Als and Greenfield Chapel within a belted collar and inscribed with a date circa 1862.

JOHN INNES' REFERENCES TO THE MAP OF

LLANELLI DATED 1860/1815

A	The Mansell Hotel.
B	The Post Office: Mr Morgan. Last Portreeve.
C	The Ship Inn.
D	John Deer's house and shop.
E	The Three Crowns Inn.
F	Charles Neville's (Elder) House.
G	Dr T. B. Cook – later moved to Pemberton Mansion, where library now stands.
H	Vicarage of Parish Church (original).
J	The Old Black Horse Inn.
K	John Howell, Surveyor, Map Maker, Parish Clerk.
L	Beehive Inn.
M	Elm Grove.
N	
O	Wesleyan Chapel (Welsh) founded By Henry Child.
P	Falcon Inn. Later to become London House. The Home of John Randall (1828-1887) and son David (1851-1912) founder of Presbyterian Church (Cowell Street).
Q	
R	The Black Bear.
S	
T	
U	Henry Child's House.
V	

CP	Cwrt-y-Plas. Courtyard of Llanelli House
2	Gelli-On Chapel.
3	Bradbury Hall. Home of J.K. Cook (1813-1859) Surgeon.
4	The Pottery.
5	Old Town Hall and Corn Market.
6	PM. Originally old pig market.
7	Caeffir (Field of the Fair) originally Old Castle Market.
8	Vicarage (New).
9	Lower Mill.
10	Upper Mill.
12	Poultry Market

9

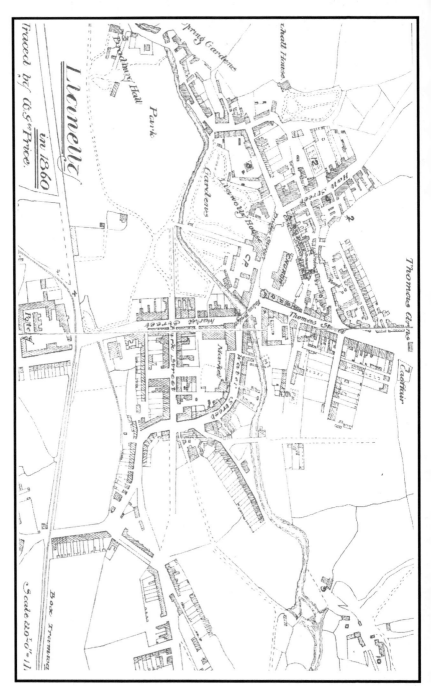

Llanelly in 1860

traced by W. G. Price.

Scale 220.0" = 1 m.

Park

Bryn bury Hall

Spring Gardens

Gardens

Llanelly House

CP

Market Street

Market Street

Thomas Arms

Castier

Box Tremerug

Pottery

10

CHAPTER THREE
DEVELOPMENT OR THE OLD TOWN PRE 1900

The early 19th century saw the start of many changes in the structure of administration and the towns environs as well as the development of industrialisation in the area. The upper and lower markets were opened, Wesleyan Chapel in Wind Street rebuilt, and building works on New Road and Hall Street commenced alongside the start of production at the Cambrian Copperworks, and by 1831 the population had risen to 7,646.

In 1835 the first floating dock in Wales opened under the New Dock banner, the Llanelly Railway and Dock Company having been previously incorporated. Finally the Gas Company was formed to provide lighting to Llanelly and its districts.

1843/1844 gave rise to the Rebecca riots, mentioned later, which provided much excitement and some disruption to life in the town which culminated in some of the toll gates in the area being demolished.

Progress of the Gas Company was leisurely, but Llanelly was beginning to see the benefits of gas lighting, and to further facilitate expansion of the town with the rebuilding of Falcon Bridge, the course of the river Lleidi was diverted above the north end of Old Castle Road, crossing the main railway line and into the dock at Raby's shipping place. The rebuilding of the old Falcon Bridge gave wider access to Bridge Street which in turn was itself widened.

The widening of Bridge Street, which took away burial space of the Parish Church, in itself congested gave rise to the establishment of two new cemeteries, one at the rear of Old Road and the other at Box in 1851. The need for this much wanted facility was obvious since the population of the town had increased by more than 30% in just over ten years to above 10,000 inhabitants. Additional developments followed with the commencement of the building of Station Road in 1845 and expansion of the Wern and Seaside districts.

1850 saw the end of the Portreve system of the local administration consisting of an undefined number of Burgesses and Trustees which had long been the subject of scathing comment in the town. As a direct result of the publication of the Clark Report by the Commissioner of the Board of Health on the sanitary conditions existing in Llanelly, theTrustees were stripped of all their duties, powers and authorities which were then vested in a new Local Board of Health of elected officers to administer all of the lands, buildings, works and duties. The change was met with enthusiastic approval by the townspeople.

To their commendation the Board set about to improve the towns facilities with fervour, recording all accounts in ledger form and opening all meetings to representatives of the press for public scrutiny.

Housing developments in Ann Street, Marine Street, New Road, Mount Pleasant and Union Building commenced, although water supply for both domestic and industrial use, sanitation and the disposal of household refuse were still of major concern.

In 1852 the first municipal Fire Engine Service started which previously had been undertaken by a small number of private engines of the industrialists and landowners. This was followed by the inauguration of the first lifeboat service at the port.

The reputation of the South Wales collier was well known throughout Britain, Europe and the Americas, so much so that they induced to emigrate to these lands on the promise of higher wages to establish new mines. There is a record of Llanelly miners among those who under the pay of the West Columbia Mining Co. sailed to New York on the "Middlesex" in December 1853.

Following a report on the towns water supply, a scheme was presented to the Board to obtain water from the catchments of Trebeddrod and the Furnace Pond; together with the construction of works to facilitate an ample supply for both domestic consumption and the removal of contaminated drain and sewerage waters. The following year in 1854 with the Board's aproval the work commenced.

By 1855 the Seaside and Wern areas finally enjoyed the benefit of gas lighting, and, due to its regional expansion the towns representation was split into three wards, each ward returning six members to the local governing Board and demonstrating that democracy to some extent was beginning to emerge in local politics.

In 1857, the Athenaeum was erected on the site of Dr B. Cook's house, which was known as "Pemberton Mansion" after Ralph Pemberton who had resided there, and the Public Baths were opened in Market Street. Improvements in the standard of the roadworks were driven by the expansion and diversity of industry within the area, but this brought with it pollution problems to the rivers in the district, namely the Dafen and Lleidi, and to the streets.

The Board resolved in July 1859 to levy a water rate instead of a special District Rate, and with it a recommendation for regular street cleaning which was duly approved. The next item on the Boards agenda was a review of the various markets which opened in the town, of which there was some half dozen, each one serving a particular need and independent of the others. Recognising that consolidation would benefit both the town and its inhabitants, the Board concluded that the market should be a public enterprise held freehold and not under the direction of private individuals.On this basis the Board applied to Parliament for full powers to provide a properly constituted market accommodation for the town. In 1864 the foundation stone was laid for the market which coincided with the opening of Park-Y-Dref, or Peoples Park, and trading opened in the market in 1866.

Over this period an extension to the Ship and Castle Hotel was completed and the areas of Stepney Street and Vaughan Street were developed, and by 1861 the part completed Neville Memorial Hall in Vaughan Street was handed over by the committee of the Board. That year saw the erection of a chimney and intake flues at the Copperworks, christened by the locals "Stack Fawr" which was to become a local landmark for many years as it stood higher than any other building, even those on high ground in the area.

From 1866 domestic waste and refuse was collected by paid employees of the Board called "Public Scavengers" whose duty it was to collect and remove the rubbish on a daily basis from wooden boxes deposited by householders outside their dwellings, and who in turn paid a charge to the Board for the service.

The first Cwm Lleidi Waterworks opened in 1869, although there had been no great improvement in the sewage disposal system whilst the population had risen to some 13,500 inhabitants. The result was inevitable and typhoid, smallpox and scarlet fever outbreaks were rife, and the urgent needs of adequate sanitation, supplies of both clean water for consumption and domestic use with that required by industry was brought before the Board. The inadequacy of supply was often critical in the drier summer months when drought conditions were imposed on the inhabitants and industries alike.

Throughout the 1870's activity in Llanelly gained momentum and Parliamentary permission was sought and granted to an Act allowing a new network of waterworks along the Lleidi valley by a diversion of the river and adaption of the upper and lower town mills at Felinfoel.

In 1872 Dr Buckley was appointed Llanelly's first Medical Officer of Health, and there followed the start of the Tuesday half day closure of the towns shops, wide expansion of local school facilities, and the erection of new churches of every denomination across the district. This activity was to continue to 1878 when one momentus day the Great Western Railway opened its passenger station in the town.

Other than the Board, the only other authority acting in Llanelly in this period was the Harbour Commission, and this too was to end in 1878 by an Act of Parliament which transferred all powers, rights and properties of the Harbour Commission to the Board of Health. Coincidentally the new Cwm Lleidi waterworks at Swiss Valley opened in the same year, and there followed the installation of sewage pipeworks through Lloyd Street and the Lakefield and Station areas, leaving only the Seaside area still totally dependent on the Board's "Watering Cart" to supply their needs. An additional branch pipeline was laid in 1880 directly to service the Felinfoel Brewery, although the total cost of this was met by the brewery.

By 1881 the Board's responsibilities were far reaching and its committees numerous, covering Highways, Sewage and General Works, Parks, Public Health and Finance, each getting in the others way for room in the cramped conditions of the Town Hall in Hall Street.

Debate on the need for a new Town Hall and its preferred location took place on many occasions after that, but nothing was resolved until the year of the first County Council elections in1889 when a site was finally agreed upon out of three locations considered, and was to be at the town end of the Spring Gardens to the west of Llanelly House.

Over this period other changes occurred which made the site more logical, the first being the proposed relocation of the main Post Office to Cowell Street. The establishment which had previously housed the functions of the Post Office numbered eight in all, from the rear of Llanelly House to the Mansell in Church Street, Thomas Street, in the Falcon the old London House, and when the Falcon moved to the site which was to become the Royalty Theatre it followed. From there it moved to the east side of the Thomas Arms, and back to Llanelly House facing the Neville Memorial Hall and on to the middle of Stepney Street. Its final move to Cowell Street being the only purpose built establishment in all its moves, and by this time the volume of business justified the support of six sub Post Offices in the districts. 1885 ended having also seen the opening of Llanelly Hospital in Marble Hall Road and all the local turnpikes abolished. To mark the golden jubilee of the reign of Queen Victoria the Parish Hall was built in 1887 as a centre of religious, cultural and social activity. The style of the building was intended to be Gothic, but apart from the entrance portico, the rest has a strong ecclesiastic influence.

The 1890's saw the beginnings of change to the administrative body of the town following the passing of the Local Government Act of 1894. The Local Board was dissolved and its functions were taken over by the Llanelly Urban District Council. Members to the Council were duly elected representatives of the three wards, each ward returning six members which duly came about following the local Borough Election in December 1894.

Earlier in the January of 1894 Mr Thomas Pugh Jones, a local building contractor was awarded the contract for the building of the new Town Hall to the design submitted by another "Llanellyite" Mr William Griffiths of Thomas Street. Work on the building was done at record pace and the new Town Hall was officially opened fifteen months later in March 1896. The opening ceremony took place with great pomp and splendour in the presence of a huge throng of spectators, reported to have been "many thousands" by some who had no way of estimating the numbers. Mrs J A Jones, wife of the Chairman of the Council, performed the opening ceremony supported by every member and local dignitary for miles around, who, after the event, attended a lavish luncheon served in the Arthenaeum Hall. A great day was had by all, and the offices of the Council duly moved from Hall Street to the splendour of the new Town Hall.

The end of the century saw the commencement of building work on the Commissioners Dock in 1898; a new administration with a town having a population of more than 20,000, and the continuing arguments, frequently heated, on the merits for and against the adoption of Municipal Incorporation which had raged for more than sixty years.

CHAPTER FOUR
THE GROWTH OF RELIGION

As early as the mid 1660's non-conformist religions were active in and around the Llanelly area, being mainly Baptists that held their meetings in "preaching stations" throughout Carmarthenshire. The earliest date of reference to a Chapel however was that of a trust deed relating to the Adulam Baptist Chapel at Felinfoel in 1709, and from which in 1718 a series of Baptist associations were recorded.

In 1768, whether by invitation or not isn't recorded, the Rev. John Wesley made the first of six visits to preach in the town. There was a small number of converts to the Wesleyan form of worship already resident in the town, some in the employ of Sir Thomas Stepney, before that date.

During his visits he would often stay at the residence of the Deers who owned a house and shop in Church Street, and as regularly entertained at the table of Henry Child and his wife at their home in Thomas Street. The station chosen by John Wesley to deliver his teachings and sermons was to the west of the lych gate of the Parish Church, set at the junction of Church and Bridge Streets, with the stocks facing him on the opposite side of the entrance.

John Wesley's last visit to Llanelly was in 1788, but his influence in his association with Henry Child fostered in the latter the desire to build the first Welsh Wesleyan Chapel at Llanelly. With the help of some others of like mind the first building of Wesleyan worship was erected in a detached plot of Mr Child's garden which in 1792 extended from Thomas Street to Wind Street. After the death of Mr Child in 1824 the Chapel was gifted to the Wesleyan Body who rebuilt it in 1828 and further enlarged it in 1834.

During this period other denominations were also established, with the first Independent Chapel, Capel Als, in 1780, at the bottom of Marble Hall Road, and five years later a Calvinistic Methodist Chapter at Gelli On, and in 1793 a second Wesleyan Chapel was built in Wind Street. There followed a fallow period until 1822 when the Baptists established Zion Chapel in the town, which was followed by another Baptist Chapel "Zoar" at Llwynhendy in 1830 and an Independent Chapel in Park Street in 1839.

The Independent Congregational Church in Park Street deserves some special mention as it came as something of a culture shock to the church going community of Llanelly. It came about by an idea of the Rev. David Rees, pastor of the Welsh Congregational Church Capel Als. He, in recognition of the spiritual needs of a group of English speaking members of his flock, in the main families who had migrated to the area in pursuit of employment such as those at the pottery in 1829, decided to conduct one service in English at Capel Als every Sunday. This practice was to continue up to 1839, but was not well received by the Welsh speaking congregation nor yet did it serve the needs of the English element.

It was cordially agreed that there was a need for an English speaking Chapel in Llanelly, which with the assistance of the Rev. Rees was achieved with the opening of the Park Street Chapel which later became part of the Park Congregational Church built in Murray Street in 1866.

Capel Newydd, a Calvinistic Methodist Church in Felinfoel Road was rebuilt in 1840, followed by the founding of two Baptist chapels, Adulam in Felinfoel and Bethel, and the Independent Siloah.

In 1845 the disciplines of Brigham Young arrived in South Wales to preach the Mormon faith, during which they visited Llanelly. These Latter Day Saints set about converting the inhabitants, in particular the mineworkers families, with ritual baptism at night in the Lleidi River near the Old Castle. They made little headway with Welsh speaking population generally, although it is reported that a small number of converts did emigrate to North America,and following a convention at the Atheneaum, a chapel was established at Island Place. Being short lived little of its history is known as none was recorded.

Some ten years passed, then in 1856 the Wesleyan Chapel in Hall Street opened, and in 1858 St. Mary's Roman Catholic Church was built in Lloyd Street. This was followed closely by the Calvinistic Methodist Trinity Church, Holy Trinity at Felinfoel and another English Baptist, Greenfield Church.

No other addition to the church register was recorded until 1869 when St. Peter's Church was consecrated and Bethania Baptist Church was formed. In 1873 the English Presbyterian Church opened in Stepney Street and the foundation stone of the Tabernacle Independent Chapel laid.

By 1880 it would appear that Llanelly was well endowed with places of religious pursuit, and the following year saw the first Religous Census undertaken. The then editor of the Llanelly Guardian who instigated the Census requested each Church of every denomination to record and publish their attendance figures on a given Sunday.

His summary of the figures produced gave the following analysis:-

Denomination	Seating Capacity	Actual Attendance
Baptist	5550	2890
Congregationalist	5600	2650
Church of Wales	3100	1233
Calvinist	4200	1153
Wesleyan	1460	224
Roman Catholic	250	110
Latter Day Saints	130	48
Totals	20290	8407

The only conclusions which may be drawn from this census are that even in those days the churches were only half full at best, and that more than half the population were heathens.

Whilst this comment may be considered cynical to some, it does not reflect on the religious determination of the churches and their leaders. They provided adequate room and encouragement to the population to fill their church, but this in itself gave cause to friction between the denominations which is well documented by John Innes in his book Old Llanelly. Reading this serves to give a better understanding of why the present day deep rooted troubles in Ireland persist.

CHAPTER FIVE
YEARS OF CHANGE

Returning to the more basic daily lives of the working population of the area , and in particular the agricultural element, who from the beginning of the 19th century had suffered great hardship in their struggle for survival.

Small farmers, lot holders and farm labourers suffered the most, with little finance and poor facilities theirs was a constant struggle to support their families. What they did produce for sale at the markets was devalued by having to pay tolls on entry to the town.

There was no avoiding the system, as like many other towns Llanelly was encircled by a number of Toll Gates and Bars, which were administered by the various Road Trustees. Charge was made for carriage of all kinds, including passengers, animals and goods of every type. Gates were open daily but closed at night when the validity of the daily ticket was deemed to expire at midnight.

By 1842 anger against the tolls was reaching dangerous proportions and the Road Trustees met on numerous occasions to resolve the conflict. At one point they offered a feeble gesture of appeasement by allowing carriage of all lime for use in agriculture to be transported through the gates free of charge. This did little to pacify the farmers, and there followed a series of cases of arson directed at the major landowners who profited from the tolls.

The farmers too held meetings, one such on Mynydd Sylen in the hills was said to have been attended by more than 4,000 incensed supporters although the meeting in general was reported to have been conducted in a law abiding and orderly fashion. The result of the inability to defuse the situation resulted in the formation of groups of conspirators being formed under a leader whose purpose was to attack, destroy and generally take revenge for the objects and individuals recognised as the perpetrators of their plight.

The leader of each group, a man dressed outwardly as a woman wearing a white cloak and generally astride a white horse was christened Rebecca. Other members of the group called the "Daughters" similarly dressed as women wearing an overshirt of white, with many having their faces blackened to avoid identification. Most sported guns or horns, although the purpose of these was for creating noise and confusion rather than anything more sinister.

They attacked the objects of their anger, the Toll Gates, at night, but it would seem with great consideration for the toll-keeper and his family who were but minions of the owners. It was reported on one occasion that having stormed the area surrounding a toll gate, the conspirators assisted the toll-keeper in the removal of his possessions before setting fire to the toll house.

In this manner the Llanelly tollgates at Furnace Gate and Sandy Gate were demolished in August of 1834, together with a conflict at the Hendy Gate in which more seriously the toll-keeper was killed and the militia called out to deal with the affray. There followed at the Carmarthen Assizes the trial of the ringleaders of the disturbances, the two foremost in which received a sentence of one to transportation for life, and the other to twenty years imprisonment.

The only good resulting from the conflict was the formation of a rural police force under the direction of the towns' Police Station.

Improvements in the methods of mining coal in the area brought with it the benefit of attracting other types of industry. The earliest of these was in 1802 when the Foundry and Engineering Works of Mr H. Waddle was established at the North Dock and later moved to a new site at the Wern. Lead smelting began in the North Dock in 1815.

In 1830 the English Copperworks Co established the Cambrian Copperworks, which alongside their developing interests in coal, they operated there until 1841. Following its closure and conversion to a lead and silver operation, the works reopened in 1849 under the management of Neville Druce & Co.

To 1850 and the following years there was massive investment in the tinplate industry giving rise to the establishment of many works in the area. The fortunes of each were as the vagaries of the weather and it is simpler to list at this juncture their emergence, to name a few:-

The Dafen Works 1846
The Morfa Tinplate Works 1852
Old Lodge Works 1853
The Glanmore Iron Works (with the first blast furnace) 1854
Morewood Works 1860
Marshfield Works 1862
The Old Castle Works 1866/67
South Wales Works at Machynys 1872
Thomas and Clements Foundry Works 1874
The Bury Tinplate Co at Machynys 1875
Western Tinplate Works(later took over the Marshfield) 1888
Yspyty Works at Bynea 1892

During a short period from 1889 industry was to benefit from electric lighting installed first in the South Wales Works, The Western, Old Lodge and others quickly followed.

After the turn of the century industry in Llanelly supported the families of more than 5,000 employees. The manufacture of tinned plate is reserved for special mention in the annals of the industrial development of Llanelly as it not only brought together an alliance of diverse industries, but also affected lives and fortunes of its workers such was its vagaries, and the total dependence of its employees.

The tinning of iron was a process known well before it appeared locally as patents of the process were filed in Britain as early as 1690. Small plants or mills abounded in the South Wales area mainly for reasons of its proximity to the basic materials used in its production. Tin from the Cornish mines, the availability of iron ore, limestone and wood for its smelters, and an abundance of rivers which provided both motive power for mills and forges and cleaning and washing processes.

The first mill in the area was opened at Kidwelly in 1738 using water as its power source, and by 1800 a number of small plants were established comprising a forge, mill stand and tinning house powered by steam.

The emergence of canned packaging in the processed food distribution saw the industry flourish and Welsh tinplate satisfied the demands of the rest of the industrial world. Monopoly of the market did little for the longer term development into a large scale processing industry as it gave rise to a reluctance to change from the old methods of manufacture. Change however was forced upon the industry between 1870 and 1890 when steel was introduced to replace iron in the tinning industry forcing the closure of the old iron forges.

A crucial blow befell the tinplate industry in 1893 which brought the South Wales manufacturers to their knees as, America, who at the time accounted for some 75% of Welsh tinplate production, imposed an import tariff on tinplate to protect their own manufacture which was emerging. It was this, together with the obsolescence of the hand mill process saw the decline and ultimate demise of the old system in the early years of the twentieth century, bringing with it extreme misery and hardship to those employed in Welsh manufacturing and a decline in the economy on a wide scale.

Local casualties of this depression began with the closure of the Bury works, closely followed by other small manufacturers. These were bought out by Richard Thomas & Co, who by 1898 had acquired nineteen of the sixty mills in the original group manufacturing in the area. Included to in acquisitioning was the foundry and steelworks of the South Wales Works at Machynys.

On a municipal front leading up to this period Llanelly had not been delinquent in its progress, 1885 saw the opening of the first purpose built regulated hospital at the top of Marble Hall Road, it replaced an establishment comprising three converted cottages at Bygyn Park Terrace near the top of Bygyn Hill which had been established in 1867. The new hospital with its imposing Gothic Style entrance was funded by public and private donation, the children's ward was donated by Mrs Buckley the widow of Dr Buckley, a feature of which was a series of panels made of ceramic tiles depicting scenes from well known nursery rhymes. Thankfully these have been saved to be preserved in the later Prince Philip hospital which serves Llanelly in the present day.

By this time too, Llanelly's first telephone exchange had been established in the town the Postal Authority having established in 1884 the pledge of sufficient subscribers to warrant its installation.

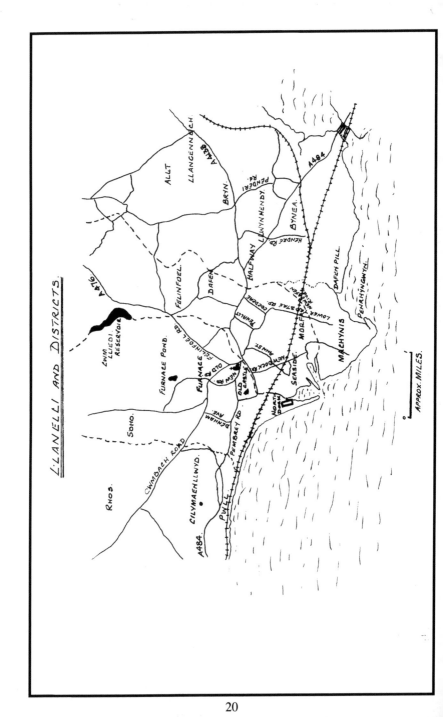

LLANELLI AND DISTRICTS.

APPROX. MILES.

CHAPTER SIX
OF BEER AND COMMERCE

At first sight the brewing of ale would seem to have little to ally the production to the heavy industry of the area, other than its consumption in large quantities to slake the thirst of the hardworking miners and tinworkers. Closer inspection shows that there were much greater commercial links between them. Early records show that there was a small brewhouse alongside the River Lleidi upstream of the Falcon Bridge on the north bank.

The Buckleys Brewery enterprise came about by the inspiration of Henry Child who worked as an estate agent for Sir Thomas Stepney. In 1769 he leased the Talbots Head Inn and the Falcon Inn, the latter included in the land on which the old Malt House was situated. Child's vision was that by controlling a business including its fringes from start to finish would magnify his profit many times.

On this premise he went on to lease local arable farmland to grow barley and wheat, leased the Llanelly Mill and bought the Felinfoel Mill. With these moves he effectively took over the local flour market, and controlled the main ingredient for breadmaking, together with secure supplies for his public houses. As his production increased he found that he had surplus to his local needs and promptly took a wharf at Llanelly Dock which enabled him to export his surplus. In so doing his empire infrastructure was protected as was his independence from potential suppliers. He operated too only in areas where there was a steady demand enabling him to remain profitable.

Henry Child was an associate of the Deer family and possibly through them he met the Rev John Wesley whom he later often entertained at his home. It is most probable that it was the charismatic John Wesley who may have converted Child to the Methodist preaching, as he went on to become a leader of the local society and founded the first Methodist Chapel in the town.

Other itinerant preachers visited the town over the years, and in 1794 one James Buckley based at Swansea arrived in what can only be described as a distressed state. Having attempted to cross the Lougher River he was overtaken by the strong currents but thanks to the assistance of some locals he was dragged clear although "exceeding wet and nigh on drowned". Happily he arrived at Mr Child's residence with no lasting affect from his ordeal. He made frequent visits over the next four years, at which time he married Henry Child's daughter Maria. The couple moved to a number of missions in England until 1823, when prompted by Henry Child's ill health they returned to Wales. Child died a year later and James Buckley's family took over his interests, but as Buckley was to continue with his ministry, it fell to his two sons to administer the complex business interests of the Childs Estate.

James, the second son of the Reverend Buckley took on the running of the brewery, and under his iron hand turned the enterprise into a highly successful business. On his death in 1883 control was handed to his two sons James and William Joseph who further expanded the business by the takeover of the Carmarthen United Brewery in 1890.

The business was by now highly profitable and in 1894 it became a limited company which owned or leased 120 public houses, and was selling its beer across mostly every corner of South Wales from Pembroke in the west to Maesteg in the east.

As with many of the notable families of Llanelly, the Buckleys too had a hand in the social development of the town. James Buckley Wilson, a grandson of the Reverend Buckley, who practised as an architect in Swansea was a major influence in the design of Bryncaerau Castle (Mansion House at Park Howard). A later member of the family, J.F.H.Buckley then chairman of Buckleys Brewery who sold the Mansion and grounds of what was to be Park Howard to Sir Stafford Howard to allow him to present his purchase as a gift to the town to commemorate his wedding in 1912.

Considering the business interests of the Buckleys, an amusing rider was added to the sale and gift was that the sale of alcohol at the Mansion was forbidden for its duration.

Alongside that of Buckleys Brewery, a second brewery emerged in competition, sited at Felinfoel. The Felinfoel Brewery was founded by David John, the son of Llewellyn John a local self made businessman and benefactor. Having taken over his fathers business interests in some of the iron and tinplate works in the area, he bought the old coaching inn the Kings Head lying adjacent to the toll-gate and opposite his house "Pantglas" in the village of Felinfoel in the mid 1830's. This was of course the time of "Rebecca and her Daughters", and the proximity of the toll-gate must have been of some concern to David John as he promptly renamed his acquisition "The Union".

The beer brewed by the"Union", bearing in mind that at that time almost every public house brewed its own ale, became so popular that it was sold to other local pubs for resale in preference to their own. Ultimately the demand became so great that David John was moved to build an imposing stone brewery in the grounds of his house in 1878. The Brewery straddled the River Lleidi which still runs through its premises today.

Investment in the Company in 1880 in laying pipework to supply water for the brewing process proved to be barely adequate, and in 1908 attempts were made to sink a well at the brewery. The scheme, no doubt fostered by the fact that David John's family held mining interests, came unstuck when some 35 feet below the surface his workmen struck a coal seam. Happily for the brewery its owners decided not to explore their new found coal mining potential and the Brewery remained intact.

To the roots of the establishment of a Chamber of Commerce in the town little can be added to those recorded by John Innes despite the efforts of historians since. In his book "Old Llanelly" he intimates that the date would appear to have been in the early 1840's, and that the earliest of the recorded minutes of a meeting dated back to 1847 during the time which H.M.Treasury conferred on Llanelly the privileges of a bonded port.

Like many other facets, over the years there have been many changes in the trends of shopping in the town and districts occasioned by the decline of the "family concerns" and redevelopments in the area. No one today will remember Herberts the Draper, Wades Chemist, Aucklands Boot and Shoemakers or Tom and Walter Davies's Cycle Shop in Stepney Street in the 1880 to 1890's.

The last mentioned being the inspiration behind the invention of the "Stepney Spare Wheel" which they later patented and manufactured at their factory in Copperworks Road in 1906. The brothers also owned a taxi service, and the idea was born out of the need to keep the cab roadworthy following a puncture of one of its tyres. The device, a clamp-on arrangement to the damaged wheel was taken up by vehicle manufactures all over the world and was the forerunner of the car spare tyre we know today.

Some of the young business ventures were to survive to the twentieth century and beyond, Tom Morgan the Undertaker, Donoghue the fruit and vegetable merchants, Pugh Brothers Furnishers and Undertakers to name a few. The last two had warehouse facilities in Princess Street, which on more than one occasion suffered the loss of their stock due to serious fires. The undertakers service of Pugh Brothers is hardly remembered today, but it was the concern that provided the funeral arrangements for Jack John and Leonard Worsell, the first casualties of the railway riots of 1911.

Stepney Street through to the 1960's developed as the nucleus of the town for a variety of reasons, being the main thoroughfare and shopping area it was also a social magnet. Thirty years earlier, although the shops were closed, Stepney Street would be thronged with the younger element of the town. They would stroll leisurely down one side from the Presbyterian Church to Park Street and return in the same fashion on the opposite side of the road. The process was repeated a number of times during the evening, its purpose having one aim, that to meet friends and attract members of the opposite sex. Over the years the practice became known as the "Monkeys Parade".

In those years there were many varied and colourful shops along the length of Stepney Street, from large family concerns to small single fronted establishments. The Bradford House owned by the Jones family boasted 24 departments from millinery, drapes, clothing and light furnishings and also a carpet shop on the opposite side of the road.

Morris The Realm which opened in 1910 was similar in style and goods to the Bradford House and had a stronger bias to ready made clothing, toys and household articles. It had the advantage of a department which produced their own decorative trimmings particularly for millinery, and also supported a scheme for training shop assistants. It was to go the way of others however, as it was taken over in 1956 by Macowards a Cardiff based firm who eventually closed the business in 1967.

Well before this many of the older shops changed hands, and the names of many like Liptons and Peglers the Grocers, Stanley Pearce and Chidzoys the fruit and vegetable sellers, Owens the butchers and James the tailor were to be lost forever.

The market stallholders too suffered a similar fate, one well remembered was the old gentleman who sold umbrellas and walking sticks near the entrance. His stall bristled with walking aids, the handles of which were carved in the most delicate manner of birds and animals. His name too is lost to me today.

Pre 1900 the town of Llanelly was as well served by hotels and public houses as it was by churches, although it has to be acknowledged that they did not have the same seating capacity. Many of the establishments had been adapted from houses designed simply for habitation. Within the town boundaries alone there were 120 licensed premises in 1897, which as with the shops were to disappear in the development of the town in later years. Over the years too the names of some of the "pubs" have changed and other new "watering holes" have opened whose appearance and style reflected the social preferences of the period. A list of the public houses of 1897 is appended, and it is left to the reader to follow with some nostalgia those fortunate to have survived through the twentieth century.

Llanelly's entry into the early 20th century was if anything a stumbling affair. The town now dependent upon non ferrous and process industry as the main employers following the decline of the coal and copper industries needed a large injection of investment in modernisation. As a consequence external influences were to have a much greater impact on the development of the town and the quality of life of its inhabitants.

The North Dock opened in 1903, and tinplate manufacture did show some expansion albeit intermittent with exports to foreign markets, and the following year the South Wales Power Company bought out the old Tramways Company making way for the new trolley bus system.

The religious revival of 1905 was conducted with great fervour, none more so than by Llanelly's oldest chapel Adulam in Felinfoel. The Baptist minister, the Rev Benjamin Humphreys was reported to have baptised 92 individuals in one Sunday in the Weir Pool of the Lleidi. Baptism at the Weir Pool had been practised for nearly a century, but never before had such numbers been immersed regardless of season or weather in the often icy waters.

In 1909 the American Can Company began developing a can for the purpose of transporting and selling beer in small quantities. This was a complex endeavour as the can would have to withstand the pressurisation of the beer and would not adversely affect the taste and consistency of its contents. The company concluded that the can would have to be lined internally and so set about developing it. This was later to have a significant effect on both the tinplate and brewing industries in South Wales.

Between 1910 and 1911 the new YMCA building was founded in Stepney Street, the new impressive Post Office officially opened, and Llanelly's fourth cinema the Palace Theatre on the corner of Murray Street and Market Street. The cinema was never called by that name, but always "Vints" after its proprietor Leon Vint who managed to obtain a stage play licence despite the vociferous objections of the proprietor of his nearest rival Mr Haggar who owned the Hippodrome.

CHAPTER SEVEN
THE RAILWAY RIOTS

Whilst on the surface Llanelly, with a population of 32000 inhabitants was a thriving established town with export links across the industrial world, below the surface it seethed with agitation. Poverty caused by low wages and insecure employment, deprivation in poor sanitation and little health care brought rebellion flooding to the surface.

The Trimsaran miners took strike action, and the gasworks employees threatened to follow amongst the demand for a minimum wage to compensate for the rise in the cost of living against wages which had remained static since 1900. Within a short period there were seamen and dockers strikes across the country, but for Llanelly what brought it to a head was the railway strike.

The Llanelly riots took place on the 19th August 1911 following the first national railway strike in Britain. Innocuous in itself the call to strike came to the 500 plus employed by the railway on Thursday 17th August, immediately pickets were formed at the two main station gates which resulted in two passenger trains being held up at the eastern crossing. As time passed others, mainly tin workers joined the pickets in support of their cause.

At the time of the disruption the Police Force at Llanelly was reduced to fewer than twenty men, as a large number had been deployed to Tonypandy and Cardiff where it was thought these depots would see greater disruption. As a benovelent gesture by the pickets one train carrying mail, and another, a cattle train from Ireland was allowed to pass through the blockade during the night, the latter to avoid undue distress to the animals aboard.

Thomas Jones a local J.P. was instructed to proceed to the station at 5am where he was advised that soldiers stationed at Cardiff were en route to the town. A detachment of 127 men of the North Lancashire Regiment under the command of Captain Burrows arrived at 7,45 am, and by midday the early arrivals were supported by the return of Police Officers from Cardiff. A rear guard arrived at 6pm being a detachment of the Devon and Worcester Regiments, who with the North Lancs took up position along the track at each end of the station. Following this manoeuvre trains did pass through but most were pelted with stones during their passage. At around 2.30pm on Saturday the Cardiff train left Llanelly travelling west, and halted some 600 yards down the line where it was boarded by a party of the strikers who immobolised the engine. Within minutes eighty soldiers descended on the scene carrying rifles with bayonets fixed. Stones were hurled at the soldiers, and the officer in charge whose attention had been drawn to a group of civilians in the embankment gardens of Number 4 and 6 High Street gave the order to fire in that direction. The result of this action was two civilians dead, one seriously wounded, and one with a less serious gunshot wound in the hand.

Whilst this caused a temporary halt to the affray by early evening the strikers were once again massing. More in the manner of individual sorties, looting broke out on individual stores and at the home of individuals having interest in the railway. At the goods sheds where near a hundred trucks were housed, looting was systematically carried out, and one goods van containing the kit and provisions of the military looted and destroyed.

Meanwhile large groups had gathered in the main streets throughout the area, forcing the soldiers to deploy to disperse the antagonists who continued their looting. Between 11 and 11.30pm two explosions occurred in the goods yard probably caused by acetylene containers exploding in the heat of the goods vans which had been set alight. The explosions claimed the life of one cicilian and injured three others, and efforts to quell the flames by the fire brigade were hampered by the time it took to locate sufficient water power to bring the blaze under control.

By 2am on Sunday 20th August the confrontation and the strike were effectively over. Tuesday of the following week saw the burial of Jack John and Leonard Worsell the early casualties of the riot, thousands of workers lined the route from Railway Terrace, through Stepney Street and up Swansea Road to the cemetery. The coffins of the deceased were carried all the way by their friends, flanked and followed by hundreds of mourners, passing works and shops closed in sympathy and respect for the bereaved families.

CHAPTER EIGHT
THE WAR YEARS

Within local government the contentious issues of incorporation were still being debated, the committee which had been set up in 1907 had put together a scheme which was finally lodged with the Privy Council by 1912. Late in 1911, Sir Stafford Howard married Miss Muriel Stepney and was appointed Charter Mayor in anticipation of the schemes approval by the Privy Council, although formal proclamation of the Charter of Incorporation did not take place at the new Town Hall until Saturday 20th August 1913.

Serious flooding had again disrupted the town in 1912, but the inhabitants did benefit in other ways. Park Howard with its Mansion House was bequeathed to the town, and the Llanelly Cinema and Astoria Theatre opened. The towns streets were lit by electricity and the electric trolley bus system linked to Bynea and the first local bus system was established.

In celebration of the town's incorporation Lady Howard presented another gift to the town in the form of a Coat of Arms and Badge, and the town showed signs of climbing out of the doldrums of earlier years. The enthusiasm was short lived however as the First World War erupted to shatter the peace of Llanelly and the country at large. Trading naturally was to be difficult through the war years with growing shortage of materials and skilled labour depleted by enlistment. In 1915 the Mansion House at Park Howard was converted to a temporary hospital for war victims, and the following year the death of Sir Stafford Howard was announced, a loss to the town of a dedicated servant and benefactor.

At the end of the war years life again returned to the rebuilding of industry and community life of the area, this was to be proved difficult and those that returned from action found that their endeavours in the cause of the nation had produced little to improve their lives. It fell to the Borough Council to establish ways in which to regenerate the town, no easy task as the Bill for construction of another reservoir, culverting of the River Lleidi and the construction of an enclosed market which had been lodged prior to the war was turned down in 1919. The inadequate water supply was highlighted later in the year when there followed a severe drought which lasted throughout the summer months and water restrictions were imposed.

Not to be deterred, the Borough Council approved a scheme to purchase the water supply system which had serviced the Pembrey Munitions Factory, and the Llanelly Corporation Water Act resulted in 1920. The council persevered with its municipal improvement plan as well, roads and sewers were laid in the Llanerch area, progress was made on the Capel housing scheme, Tunnel Road extended and Temple, Cedric and Derwent Streets were built.

Despite the restrictions of the war and fluctuations after, there was some expansion in the tinplate industry as the automotive, petroleum and canned food industries expanded. The coal industry received a small boost alongside, this was anthracite steam became more widely used.

1923 saw the first Honorary Freeman of the Borough conferred upon the Right Honourable David Lloyd George MP, the Welsh Prime Minister, and this was closely followed by the same honour on Lt Colonel Richard Austin Neville DSO in recognition of his war services. The early part of that year too saw the opening of the new Lougher Bridge which replaced the old wooden structure which had caused much concern in regards to its safety since the turn of the century.

The year was once again to end on a sad note when a telegraph was received announcing the death of John Innes at Whitchurch near Tavistock at the age of 70 years. The family of John Innes had previously resided in Llanelly at Greenfield Villas in Murray Street and John Innes worked as an engineer with the Copperworks Company. His son James Dickson Inneswas born on the 27th February 1887. Around 1907 the Innes family moved to "Ynys Hir" a large house in Old Road with extensive rear gardens, although James at this time was studying at the Slade School of Art in London.

Both John and James Innes were later to bring acclaim to the town, John for his services to the town and pioneering work in establishing the Llanelly Mechanics Institute, but more importantly as the author of a highly regarded history of the town under the title "Old Llanelly" in 1902.

His son James having completed his studies travelled widely during which he produced painting of international acclaim. London, Tintern, Pembroke, Llanelly, North Wales, Spain, Ireland, Morocco and Tenerife provided him with subject matter, he rarely stayed long in any location and only on rare occasions did he visit Llanelly. His paintings were regularly selected for prestigious exhibitions from New York to London and Paris, his success was marred only by ill health which followed him throughout his young life. James Innes died at the early age of 27 in a nursing home at Swanley in Kent in 1914, leaving behind a wealth of sketches, watercolours and oil paintings, some thirteen of which are now housed in the towns art collection.

The work of this prolific artist also demonstrated his appeal that in a sale in 1973 one of his paintings entitled "Llanelly Bay" was sold for the sum of £4,500.

The economic recovery hinted at in 1923 was to be short lived and by 1925 the lifeblood of the town, the tinplate industry, was again floundering putting more than five thousand of its employees out of work. The Llanelly Pottery had closed in 1923 leaving a tract of derelict buildings along Murray Street to its junction with Market Street and back along Pottery Street, doing little to enhance the appearance of the town and further swell the numbers of unemployed.

Thankfully the pottery heritage was not totally lost to the town as its merits were recognised by Miss Anne Roberts who sought the assistance of Lady Howard Stepney in 1927 to salvage the effects of the Pottery from the old site. Lady Stepney made provision for the storage of the recovered items in Llanelly House. She also undertook the difficult work of cataloguing the copperplates, moulds, pestles, pallets and various oddments of pottery that were recovered, which together with other items owned by Lady Stepney are now housed in a permanent exhibition in the museum at Park Howards Mansion House.

By 1929 the unemployment situation was again reaching record level with more than 7,000 out of work and so great was the hardship suffered by the families that Llanelly was classed as a distressed area. History was again repeated, as by an odd quirk the town was nominated to host the 1930

National Eisteddfod. In an attempt to alleviate the now national massive unemployment situation the Government released capacity for public works and civic amenities. To their credit Llanelly Borough Council lost no time in implementing their shelved development plans. Redevelopment of the Spring Gardens and culverting of the River Lleidi from Vaughan Street to Old Castle Road commenced and was finally completed in 1932. A slum clearance scheme in the old areas of Caer Elms, Forge Row, Cambrian Street, Crescent Street and Custom House Bank was started to make way for the proposed urban developments and the new development of Marble Hall Road began.

The conditions of thousands living in substandard accommodation was programmed to improve with new housing scheme to provide Council owned properties for those on the rehousing list at affordable rents. The Llanerch, Capel, Morfa, Penyfan and Heol Daniel(Felinfoel) estates were constructed in 1931, for which the occupants were charged at rates between ten and fifteen shillings per week.

The Pencoed Tinplate Company built the Bynea works in 1929 in an attempt to re-establish production in the area, the venture was doomed to failure as the demand did not materialise and production ceased in 1932, and the plant remained idle until it was acquired by Richard Thomas & Company. Outlook generally for the tinplate industry was dire and they frantically searched for avenues which would restore their fortunes.

The brewers too were not idle as they also had a vested interest in the tinplate industry, and had been monitoring the progress of the American Can Co's research, whom in 1933 ran a trial of 2000 cans of beer for sampling. Further trials followed, and following some modifications the company patented a vinglite lining for cans in 1934 under the trademark "Keglined". In 1935 the Kruger Brewery of New Jersey manufactured canned beer for public sale in Richmond, Virginia.

In the UK the main British can manufacturer, the Metal Box Company, was sceptical of the beer cans potential and were slow to react. Not so tardy was the reactions of the Felinfoel Brewery who under the manager William Rees and head brewer Sidney John had been conducting their own research and experiments. Historically, Felinfoel Brewery had marketed their products in casks and bottles, but after some trial batches the John family gave their support and canned beer was produced for sale in volume in March 1936. Obviously the families interests in the tinplate industry namely the St Davids Works at Bynea were to be involved in the scheme, it was they who produced the tinsheet for the manufacture of the first British beer cans. On its release to the public every employee of the Brewery and St Davids Works were presented with a can of Felinfoel canned ale to mark the occasion.

The Metal Box Co by this time had capitulated, and they agreed to manufacture the cans from the St Davids tinsheets. The initial design of the can which was to hold 10 ounces of ale, about half a pint, had a conical shape capped on the top with a metal "crown cork", for all the world having an appearance similar to the Brasso Metal Polish can manufactured at the time, so much so that the likeness was commented upon by the Brewery Journal.

Buckleys Brewery, Felinfoels local competitor could hardly have been welcoming in the praise of their rival, although Felinfoel would have benefited from the greater volumes of can manufacture. Buckleys in fact did not produce canned beer for public sale until a number of years later.

By 1938 the inevitability of a confrontation with Germany was apparent and the Government established a munitions factory at Pembrey, the Borough Council appointed an Air Raid Committee who directed the building of Anderson Air Raid shelters at convenient sites and issued gas masks.

Whilst Richard Thomas & Co were building up an impressive list of acquisitions, the Old Castle, Western Works, Ashburnham Co, Kidwelly Co and Teilo Co formed an alliance as the Llanelly Associated Co, the purpose of the amalgamation was to develop a process along the lines of the Steckel Mill system to replace the old Pack Mill process. Thus at the outbreak of war the local tinplate industry was effectively controlled by two companies.

The war years between 1939 and 1945 saw little in the way of development of the town, but as the conflict ended the towns first tangible links with the motor vehicle industry were established when the Nuffield Corporation sited the Morris Motors factory in Felinfoel. The factory provided great relief to the unemployed, and within a year 1000 local people were at work on its production lines.

Victory in Europe day was celebrated with great gusto following the Kings' announcement. Revellers thronged the streets and gathered around the Town Hall. Later that evening the Bullring car park near the Spring Gardens became the venue for an impromptu dance hall which carried on until the early hours of the next day.

CHAPTER NINE
THE WIND OF CHANGE

In America, which had not suffered the same privations as Britain, industry had moved on apace and amongst it the tinplate industry had become a highly mechanised continuous strip mill process producing massive volumes to supply their needs. The effect on British industries was immense, the loss of exports together with the end of contracts to supply canned beer to the armed forces cut back production to a new low. Earlier another member had joined the management of the Felinfoel Brewery through the marriage of David Johns' daughter Mary Anne to John Lewis the manager of the Wern Ironworks. At this low ebb it was decided that the head offices of the brewery would transfer to London in 1951 from where the Lewis family ran their other business interests, even though at the time the Brewery had around seventy tied public houses under its local control.

The women of Llanelly had long been lobbying for a dedicated maternity facility in the town, and in 1946 following the purchase and suitable conversion of "Glasfryn" a large house with extensive gardens opposite Park Howard on the Felinfoel Road the facility was officially opened. In April of that year there was a further boost to the unemployment situation in the area when the 25 million pound Carmarthen Bay Power Station project began at Burry Port.

Late in 1947 Llanelly caused a national stir by returning an almost totally controlled socialist council at the Borough elections against the national trend. There followed a much closer, and even warmer, co-operation between the Borough and Rural District Councils, whom had become to realise that their objectives for development in housing and employment were in parallel and better served by their joint efforts.

A similar situation arose within the steel and tinplate industries, Richard Thomas & Co amalgamated with Baldwins Limited and joined with Llanelly Associated Companies, John Lysaght Co and Guest Keen & Baldwin to form The Steel Company Of Wales in 1947 to build the Abbey Steelworks at Margam and introduce electrolytic tinning at the Ebbw Vale plant in 1948.

In 1951 the Llanelly Harbour Trust collapsed under its financial burden, the North Dock closed and all other operations undertaken by the Trust suspended. Discussions with Steel Company of Wales, the Government and local authorities of South Wales took place on a regular basis for the next four years which culminated in the opening of the Trostre Steelworks Cold Strip Mill in Llanelly in 1951 and the Velindre Electrolytic Tinplate in 1956.

At this time one of the longest serving and most influential Town Clerks, Mr Selwyn Samuel took up appointment at the end of 1952, which was to provide the town with an astute leader to boost the efforts of the local government. This appointment coincided with the inauguration of the new local bus service which replaced the trolley bus system which had operated since 1911. Earlier in the year Llanelly mourned the death of Lady Catherine Meriel Stepney, widow of the towns first mayor, a mayor in her own right and a member of one of Llanelly's oldest families.

Black and white television was a luxury to most families, but in 1952 the sales of television sets soared as this was Coronation year and sets were bought by the public so that they would be able to witness the event. Llanelly like most places throughout the kingdom staged parades, carnivals and street parties, and the celebrations culminated in a visit by the new Queen to the town on the 12th July. The following year the North Dock was reopened to house 21 of the Royal Naval Reserve Fleets tank landing craft amid rumours regarding their purpose and possible future use of the docks.

The coal industry in Llanelly received an unexpected resurgence in early 1954 with announcement that work was to begin immediately on a 7 million pound anthracite coal mining project at Cynheidre in the Five Roads district.

The Labour controlled council, steadfastly supported by the socialist working class majority of Llanelly's voters, continued their plans for improving the social and domestic facilities in the town. Areas which previously had been the derelict sites of the old works became the scene of demolition on a grand scale, notable amongst these was the Old Lodge Works with its "Stack Fawr". The site of Nevilles Foundry followed suit and out of the rubble emerged tower blocks of modern flats.

Land was acquired by the Council between Old Castle Road and the Town Hall where they planned to build the new Police Station and Post Office sorting office and administration. Detailed plans were submitted in 1956 together with an extension to the culverting of the River Lleidi along the Old Castle Road frontage. With the cost jointly financed by the Borough Council, County Council and Post Office Authority the scheme was deemed financially viable and was duly authorised. That year saw the benefit to the residents of Llanelly of the "new fangled" sodium lighting installations in the streets of the town, reportedly "well received" by the townsfolk. As was often the case, 1956 ended on a serious note when all the part time workers and 200 full time workers of the Morris Motors Plant were made redundant. The action struck fear in the hearts of the industrial workers whose past experiences saw the move as the thin edge of the wedge in a journey to join the dole queue.

Despite concerted efforts to attract more industry to the area by the Council over the next three years, little was achieved until 1959 when Crawley Industrial Products set up their plant at North Dock to manufacture mechanical mining and conveyor systems. Fortuitous in its timing, as this saw the final period of the smaller steelworks closures after the slump caused by over capacity in the steel industry.

Llanelly Steelworks was acquired by Duport Ltd, whilst Bynea Steelworks, the Old Castle Works and Pemberton Works closed down. These were closely followed by the Bury Works, Glanmorgan and Glynhir works at Pontardulais, subsidiaries of the Bynea Steel Co, which in turn proved to be the beginning of the demise of Bynea Steel Co itself and also the end of the old method of manufacture in 1961. Termination of production at the Royal Ordnance factory at Pembrey added to the numbers of the unemployed, and Llanelly was again accorded the status of an area in need of the assistance of the Governments Special Industrial Aid Scheme.

As had previously occurred following a depression in 1930, Llanelly in 1961 was again nominated as the venue for the National Eisteddfod. The Bardic

Proclamation Ceremony held in Park Howard announced the venue, and one year later the Eisteddfod opened on the Penygaer fields. Before the opening, the Stepney Memorial Gallery in the Park Howard Mansion was established, and the new Divisional Police Headquarters in Waunlanyrafon entered service. To facilitate a road widening scheme at the notorious bottleneck on Felinfoel Road through the village the old coaching inn renamed the Union Inn opposite Felinfoel Brewery was demolished.

Over the years many of the towns youngsters had been taught to swim and dive in the North Dock, but this was banned to swimmers, the beach was both polluted and dangerous so little surprise then that the highlight of Llanellys' Jubilee Year of 1963 was to be the opening of the towns first indoor swimming pool. The site of the Jubilee Pool was advantageous at the end of Park Crescent near the bus station at the centre of the town.

In further celebration of its Jubilee the Borough Council hosted an exhibition in a massive marquee on the playing fields of Peoples Park which lasted for ten days. A centrepiece of the exhibition was a stand displaying a plan and scale model of the Borough Councils' proposed town centre development scheme.

Over the passage of years disagreement between the John and Lewis families at the Felinfoel Brewery had been fierce, and this was brought to a head in 1965 when Buckleys Brewery made a bid to take over its neighbouring rival. The distant control of the Felinfoel Brewery by the Lewis family gave cause to the John family to sell out, and they were surreptitiously approached by Buckleys who wished to gain their shareholding. Subsequently the crucial eleven shares which were owned by a Lady Davies were to emerge as the deciding factor in the controlling interest. She rejected the offer by Buckleys and gave her shares to the Lewises, who formed a holding company to control the sale of shares in the event of future domestic dispute. The irony of the situation was that Buckleys ended up owning 49.5% of Felinfoel Brewery shares, one seat on the Board and very little say in the running of the Company. Many offers were made by Buckleys after that, but none were successful.

In November 1966 the proposed Town Centre Redevelopment Scheme was approved by the County Planning Committee. The ambitious scheme was wide reaching and was to include the rebuilding of the market and Public Hall, erection of the Crown Buildings and Magistrates Court, provision of a new town hall administrative building and extension to the library and new car parking facilities. This added to the approval already obtained by the Council to block up the link road between Church Street and Fredrick Street, the building of a large roundabout on the Swansea Castle square and a new bypass around the Old Church from Hall Street to Thomas Street.

With credible foresight the Borough had acquired large tracts of land of the Stepney Estate amounting to 32 acres at Park Howard and 108 acres at Cilymaenllwyd. The deal also included 476 houses, 150 business premises, garages, offices, licensed premises, churches and a bank in the precincts of the town.

Many other events took place during this period, the spelling of the name of the town Llanelly was changed to the Welsh form Llanelli for no useful purpose, and for the sake of continuity is ignored in these writings as it was to revert to its earlier spelling in later years. The old grammar school entrance examination (11 plus) was abolished, the Government Training Centre and Citizens Advice Bureau were established. On the industrial front, Ina Needle Bearings started production at their new Bynea factory, Bakery Engineering Co was established at the North Dock, J.B.Eastwood started their Chicken Broiler Plant at Pembrey and Alkaline Batteries began manufacture at Ponthenry.

Late in 1966 a report by a Welsh Studies Group was published which proposed that Llanelly under a reorganisation of Welsh Local Government should become a district to administer an area from Lougher to Kidwelly. Within this remit it would have all the powers of a borough and control the Llanelly Borough, Llanelly Rural, Burry Port Urban and Kidwelly Borough areas, encompassing a total area with around 78,000 inhabitants. There was obviously going to be a great deal of discussion and negotiation between the participants in the period between presentation of the Governments White Paper on Welsh Local Government and final approval of the Home Office.

Locally the greatest opposition to the merger was from the Kidwelly Borough, by far the oldest whose Charter reached back over 860 years, and felt it had the most to lose. Their objections were to be of no avail for although it had undoubted status, Kidwelly had little else to offer against the larger and stronger industrial and commercial interests and influences of the others. Finally Kidwelly resolved to support the overall concept contained in the White Paper, at the same time petitioning for dispensation for the town to retain its historic Charter and Borough title within the new organisation. This was ultimately granted.

In 1967 the Freedom of the Borough was conferred on Sir Fredrick Elwyn Jones QC, the then Attorney General, who went on to become Lord Elwyn. Educated in Llanelly and Cambridge before being called to the Bar at Grays Inn. After a successful career in law during which he was a member of the British War Crimes Executive at the Nuremburg Trials, he turned his attention to politics and was elected a Member of Parliament. In 1964 he was made a Privy Councillor and knighted for his services.

Late in 1968 signs of Llanelly's town redevelopment scheme began to materialise, Gelli On opened, the first new major road in more than three decades, linking Hall Street and Thomas Street to the rear of the Parish Church. The name Gelli On was resurrected from an old road which ran north from its junction with Hall Street, north of the site of the then Town Hall. How the original road got its name is unknown, but it translates into English as Ash Grove.

Activity in the proposed changes became more apparent as the multi-storey car park was constructed at the eastern end of town with an entrance ramp in Murray Street, and the new dual carriageway flanked by the British Legion Headquarters on one side and Magistrates Court and Crown Buildings on the other began to emerge on the western end.

Amongst this activity the investiture of Prince Charles as the Prince of Wales took place at Caernafon Castle and his subsequent tour of the Principality included a visit to Llanelly in July 1969. Shortly after the opening of the second multi-storey car park, Llanelly was to lose two of its oldest edifices.

The first was the Welsh Metal and Tinstamping Co, which had first set up in 1891 in Ann Street and in 1898 relocated to the old Lead Works site in Cambrian Street. The "Stamping" with its facilities for enamelling and japanning had achieved wide acclaim for its enamelware, in particular for saucepans. The association between the "Sospanites" of Llanelly and Llanelly's rugby war song "Sospan Fach" is well known throughout the rugby world, but this was to be the end of manufacture of the sign of the emblem of the morale of the town through nearly eighty years. The second loss to the town was that of the Regal Cinema which had been turned into a bingo hall was destroyed by fire during the Christmas period.

Over the four years to 1970 Felinfoel Brewery gradually modernised its plant under the direction of John Lewis. Whilst Fred Cheesewright the Head Brewer diligently worked to improve and maintain the quality of the "brew". John's father, Trevor Lewis died in 1974 and the head office of the Brewery returned to Llanelly. The efforts of these individuals together with those employed by the Company were not to be unrewarded as the Brewery was awarded the Challenge Cup for its premier bitter Double Dragon at the Brewers Exhibition in London in 1976.

Late in 1974 the Llanelly District Council applied to the Minister for the Arts for independence for the running and affairs of the Llanelly Public Library and were allowed temporary approval. Dyfed County Council wishing to have control of all of the libraries within its jurisdiction strongly opposed the application, but thanks in the main to Mr Harold Prescott the Librarian, and the support of the towns councillors the order was made permanent in February 1975. This was to prove a huge benefit to local historians, students and the general public at large, as Mr Prescotts administration had developed a well appointed library for the town, and his own tireless work in preserving and recording the events and changes to the town over the years was to provide a wealth of invaluable historical information for its archives.

The year also saw the completion of the redevelopment of the market precinct which had taken seven years to evolve from the old market pavilion. A royal visit took place in the town, occasioned this time to confer the Freedom of the Borough on the Royal Regiment of Wales. The newly appointed Regiment had evolved from the armed forces reorganisation of 1969 which amalgamated the Welch Regiment and the South Wales Borderers. The Prince of Wales as Colonel in Chief of the new Regiment arrived by helicopter to land at Peoples Park to receive the Honour whilst the Royal Regiment displayed their Colours.

The euphoria of the year was dimmed somewhat by the death of Mr Jim Griffiths at the age of 84, who had served as Llanellys Member of Parliament for thirty years during which he had been appointed the first Secretary of State for Wales.

Llanelly as a town became the proud owner of its first theatre in 1976. Having acquired the leasehold of the old Odeon Cinema built in 1938 the Council began refurbishing and refitting the building to utilise it on a commercial basis as a cinema, theatre and other community activities of an artistic nature. It was later reopened under its new name the Classic Theatre. Meanwhile proposals for the next stage of the town centre redevelopment were tabled for consideration by the Borough Council which included the demolition of the area of the junction of Market Street and Park Street to make way for the construction of the second multi- storey car park and superstore. The year ended with the announcement by the Welsh Office that approval had been granted for the construction of a new general hospital at Bryngwyn.

The silver jubilee year of 1977 was the occasion of yet another royal visit to the town. Queen Elizabeth II and Prince Philip, Duke of Edinburgh arrived in June, and were lauded all along the route from the station to Park Howard by a crowd of 20,000 or more, and met by the Borough Council and Civic Reception Committee at the Mansion House.

The following year the Council sat to consider more mundane issues, the bulwarks of the Bury Estuary between Machynys and Llwynhendy had often been breached by the tides. The bulwarks mainly of loosely packed slag from the old works were inefficient resulting in widespread flooding in the area. It was concluded that a more formal barrage would alleviate the problem, provide an area for refuse tipping which was at a premium, and ultimately open up the possibility for redevelopment of reclaimed land. The scheme was temporarily shelved as finance could not made available and no subsidy in the form of grants. A facility for the sport of skateboarding was opened in Peoples Park, but this, like other fads of the youth of Llanelly was of little long term benefit to the town.

Another milestone was reached in 1979 when the town watched the final death throes of another old established industrial concern. The 130 year old Glanmore Foundry and Engineering Works having long battled against poor investment and stronger competition went into voluntary liquidation with the loss of 170 jobs. The only glimmer of hope for the older industries was the commissioning of the new electric furnaces of the Duport Steelworks who had taken over the old Llanelly Steelworks.

The cultural facilities of the town in 1979 were added to by the establishment of the Gwyl Festival, a week long celebration of music, drama and visual arts, which it was hoped would become an annual event and encourage the participation of the younger element in the town and neighbouring areas. Its success was to depend upon the hard work of a small group of like minded individuals and the ongoing support of the Borough Council.

CHAPTER TEN
UNEMPLOYMENT IN THE 1980'S

The dilemma facing the Borough Council in 1980 with unemployment at its highest for twenty five years, was, what to allocate its depleted expenditure budget on to best effect having suffered severe cutbacks. They settled on a civic programme rather than a domestic one, and as a consequence domestic property building fell to not much more than a dozen houses and improvement grants and mortgages suffered. Boots Chemists agreed to participate in the plan to develop Stepney Street and Vaughan Street and relocated at their own expense to develop a new store opposite their old site.

With their sights fixed on the civic programme the Council failed to anticipate the industrial problems which were to fall on the town. In September the Duport Steelworks announced that a total of 575 workers were to be made redundant, and the last link with the old works was about to be severed. The Llanelly Steelworks, fondly christened "the Klondike" locally when workers rushed to enjoy higher wages at the works, had produced steel at Llanelly since the 1890's. Using the open hearth furnace method fired by a coal gas and air mixture to melt the pig iron, steel scrap, limestone and manganese which had to be hand fed by the chargers into the furnace. When fusion of the charge was complete and samples verified, the furnace was tapped allowing the molten metal to run onto a ladle which was then transported to rows of cast iron moulds which after filling were allowed to solidify. The resultant ingot weighing almost an imperial ton was then ready for rolling at the mill into pans. As the process became a little more mechanised, changing of the furnace was achieved by machinery conveying charger boxes on rail trolleys which tipped the charge into the furnace without human effort. The plant under Duport Steel finally closed down in March 1981 with the loss of 1000 jobs in the area, on top of which 350 from Buxted Poultry and Bowden Controls were added.

Whilst the official opening of the Pembrey Country Park had been a pleasant diversion for the Borough Council, they were left with a serious headache when the Government Housing Act 1980 came into force which allowed tenants to buy their council owned homes at reasonable prices. At that time the Borough Council owned nearly 10,000 houses of widely different types over a large area of its authority.

To meet the problems of unemployment the Council had began a pilot scheme at their Lower Trostre Road Industrial Estate to encourage the growth of a "cottage industry" of small units which would not have such damaging effects on the unemployment situation should they fail, and have more chance of success being independent of the results of their neighbours. Supported by a Small Business Advice Service attached to the Planning Department in Goring Road, the plan flourished.

Atrocious weather conditions prevailed in early 1982, and were so bad that the Territorial Army were mobilised to assist in maintaining links with communities cut off by snow storms which had drifted to depths of up to ten feet. They provided transport services to hospital workers, between hospital and chemists with medical supplies and delivering food and milk to isolated homes and villages. The W.R.V.S. too had their resources stretched in providing hot food to the elderly inhabitants of the town.

As the inclement weather abated the Borough Council's new Administrative Building was opened on the site of the demolished Regal Cinema. The building was named Ty Elwyn in honour of Lord Elwyn who also performed the opening ceremony in sight of his childhood upbringing in Old Castle Road.

Whilst formulating other plans for development following the success of the Lower Trostre Road scheme, the proposed Business Park at Cross Hands and South Llanelly scheme were progressing. The large tracts of land between Pond Twyn, the old water discharge catchment of the Old Castle Tinplate Works and the old path to the beach at Pwll served only as a reminder of the industries that had once been the life blood of the town.

In January 1983 Llanelly mourned the passing of one of Wales' rugby legends, Carwyn James had died on the 15th of the month whilst on holiday in Holland. Having played as a youth for the Scarlets and gaining three schoolboy caps, he went on to win two senior international caps for Wales. Later he coached the Scarlets between 1967 and 1975 and the British Lions triumphant tour of Australia and New Zealand in the 1970/1971 season. He was widely acclaimed as one of the best rugby strategists and coaches ever in Welsh rugby history.

A further loss to the town, although not in the same vein, was the retirement of Mr H.A.Prescott the Borough Librarian of 33 years who had done much to preserve the history of the town for following generations. Llanelly workshops at Trostre Road officially opened its start up units for local individuals wishing to set up in business, and the Llanelly Enterprise Company was formed to establish counselling services and lease and manage the complex for the potential business entrepeneurs. The need for this service became even more apparent when the closure of the Carmarthen Bay Power Station closed in October adding even further to the unemployed in the area.

Further redevelopment of the town area was evident in 1984 when another landmark disappeared when Coleshill Secondary School which had served the town since 1891 was demolished. Whilst "Cor Meibion" Llanelly's celebrated male voice choir was taking top honours for the first time at the National Eisteddfod, held at Lampeter, the ominous signs of industrial unrest erupted with the start of the miners strike.

1985 was once again one of the disaster years for unemployment in Llanelly, whilst the miners continued their strike, Machynys Foundry closed and their were redundancies at the L.R.Industries factory at Bynea. On top of these disappointments, Llanellys status as a development area was inexplicably withdrawn and with it support for the Skill Centre, causing its closure. Given that unemployment in the Borough hovered between 19% and 20% at the time the administrators and inhabitants of Llanelly must have felt they were running into a brick wall of bureaucracy.

The Borough Council could only concentrate its efforts in tourism, with craft fairs and events at the Pembrey Country Park, and town developments which were well advanced like the Wern scheme. The St. Pauls' School conversion to sheltered accommodation for the elderly opened at the end of the year.

News of the proposal of the Borough Council's action to consideration to develop a retail park on the outskirts of the town at Trostre was met by the local town centre shopkeepers and Chamber of Commerce with vocal expression of deep concern in February 1986. Previously there had been heated dissent by these groups regarding the high rates and rental costs in the new market area, and they felt that this new move would draw away custom from the town and impair the profitability of the town centre trade.

The Borough Council were not to be distracted on this issue, and concerned themselves instead with its plan for the Old Castle and Duport area which, with the aid of a grant from the Welsh Development Agency, it now owned and would in the future become part of a much larger scheme for the whole of the coastal length of its authority. The only distraction to the inhabitants of the town was Llanelly's first "fun run" through the streets which it was hoped would encourage a healthier life style and an annual event in the town in the future, and the beginnings of the Welsh Motor Sport Centre at the abandoned chicken factory site at Pembrey.

At the end of the miners strike following a visit of Arthur Scargill the President of the N.U.M., the Borough Council allowed a pilot scheme in Cowell Street and lower Stepney Street to gauge reaction to street stall marketing, the reactions of the inhabitants was mixed to say the least. At the Dafen Industrial Park occupancy of the advance factories had been slow with only Avon Rubber its committed incumbent.

Mid year saw redundancies at the British Optical plant at Kidwelly, followed by news that the large Pressing Plant at Felinfoel could be closed by 1987. Generally 1986 was a year which could only be described as one of uncertainty, rumours were rife, one of which was that the takeover of Buckleys Brewery. At the time less than 40% of the shareholding was held by the management and local investors in the Brewery, the balance being with Whitbread and Scottish Brewers, Brittanic, Guardian, Scottish Amicable, Co-op and Royal Exchange Assurance Companies, the N.C.B.Pension Fund and County Bank Investments. With 17.4% held by Whitbread, the largest holding, any move by them would effect the future of the Brewery.

Early in 1987 Llanelly Borough Council unveiled their immediate plans for attracting tourism to the area within the outline ongoing scheme. They were the landscaping of Kidwelly Quay, and restoration of a section of the historic Kymer Canal which dated back to 1779 between Kidwelly and Carway. This was to be followed by the provision of a new low water launching slipway at Burry Port, and added attractions of a model boat lake, pitch and putt course and miniature railway system at Pembrey Country Park. Closer to the town the old Trebeddrod Reservoir above Furnace received a facelift, with resurfaced pathways and the remodelling of the discharge culvert into a series of water courses to fall some thirty feet below.

The skill centre which had closed early in 1985 was reopened as the Community Resource Centre for the training and retraining of adult workers, and the Flower Festival was revived after a lapse of thirty five years. Not so fortunate was the swimming fraternity, as a serious fire at the Jubilee Pool brought to a temporary halt their leisure pursuits. The year was to end on a more pleasant note however with the visit of the Prince of Wales, on this occasion to present awards to three local teams who had participated in the Prince of Wales Community Welfare Venture Scheme.

The Heir Apparent was becoming a regular visitor to the town, and was to return in the following year. 1988 was the 75th year of Llanellys' Incorporation, and the Prince of Wales visit included his attendance at the official opening of the Industrial Museum at Kidwelly. The museum had been established in the old Kidwelly Tinplate Works converted for the purpose and to preserve one of the only remaining examples of the old methods of manufacture in the United Kingdom.

Six of the old mills with their vertical steam driven engines and flywheels, together with the almost complete black pickling plant had been found to be in excellent condition and needing little refurbishment to bring them into working order. Added to this was an old saddle-tank locomotive of the 1878 era, and later the engine and winding gear from the Morlais Colliery at Llangennech. A shunting engine was acquired from a Clydach Tinplate plant, together with a locomotive complete with its attendant rolling stock from the Carmarthen Bay Power Station which made up an impressive display of the old industrial heritage. It can only be hoped that future years will see additions to the preservation of relics of the traditions, culture and industries of Wales in the same manner.

The two years prior to the last decade of the 20th century saw the commencement of trading at the Trostre Retail Park with its relocation of the towns' largest superstore from its town centre site to the larger premises with greater car parking at the out of town complex. The move, as anticipated with consternation by the towns retail shopkeepers also caused a problem for the Council who now had a large unoccupied property within the inner town area. With fortuitous intervention the independent TV programme producers Agenda took the decision to relocate their operation to the building with financial support of Carmarthenshire County Council and the Welsh Development Agency.

Penclacwydd Wildfowl Centre opened with its lagoon and hide observation together with the sanctioning of plans for the development of Park Street through Island Place with a view to extending town centre shopping. Following a merger with Crown Brewery the old established Buckleys Brewery became Crown Buckley in 1988, which continued to produce beer but managed from Cardiff, to leave Llanelly with the one remaining local producer, Felinfoel Brewery.

Meanwhile at the other end of town the Duport Lake Scheme opened and landscaping of the surrounding areas progressed, along the north shore the site was being prepared for the first phase of a new private housing development and large family style public house and restaurant. The Jubilee Pool officially reopened in March 1989.

CHAPTER ELEVEN
THE 1990'S A BLUEPRINT FOR CHANGE

The 1990's were to be a period of intensive planning for the Borough Council as the climax of the century was to bring together two major events to the town. The first was to participate in the 1999 World Rugby Cup Series in which Stradey Park was to be a venue for one of the play offs, and the second, to host the year 2000 National Eisteddfod of Wales. To enable this to happen the Council had to ensure that their bids would convince the Committees that they had the facilities to ensure the success of these prestigious events above all others competing.

In 1990 the Borough Council introduced the Community Charge, a totally new concept to local government in the area of finance, much to the dislike of most householders. With Llanellys'new Prince Philip Hospital officially opened at Bryngwyn, sadly without the hard fought maternity facility, the Cross Hands Business Park opened in May, and both went on to prove an outstanding success. It was to be a year of official openings starting with that of the Sandy Water Park and ending with the completion of phase 2 of the Llanelly Business Workshops.

Early in 1991 the long awaited Penclacwydd Wildfowl Centre opened which was to serve as an observatory for all age groups to study both the indigenous species and migratory wintering wading birds drawn to the area. Dafen Pond overgrown and long forgotten with its early links was finally restored to take its place as a nature conservation area.

Following a review of the now wide ranging activities of the Borough Council a restructuring of its organisation was agreed to allow the Authority to more closely follow its aims with directors to head each section. In part this would also fill the gaps where a number of the older Chief Officers had elected to retire and streamline the structure.

Phase II of the Sandy housing development continued and continual progress was being made on the coastal link road as sections were opened. One of particular benefit was the section which ran from the end of Queen Victoria Road to the Trostre roundabout, effectively giving relief to the town centre in a bypass for heavy traffic for 1993. Following the reduction in the number of council owned housing stock to some 6500 homes through sales to tenants, the Authority turned its attentions to the emerging problem of more appropriate accommodation for the growing number of dependent elderly citizens. Sheltered housing schemes were embarked on at Llangennech, Dafen, Seaside and Cefncaeau.

In 1993 the ski slope and toboggan run were officially opened at Pembrey Country Park following that of a new restaurant. Within the town the frontage of the Theatre Elli, the town's entertainment centre, was redesigned to provide it with a 1930's style frontage more in keeping with the age of the building. The effect was opposite to that at the market entrance where in Vaughan Street new walkways were laid and canopies erected along part of its length. September of that year was again to see the popular Flower Festival to be held in the Peoples Park, attended by gratifying large numbers of exhibits and visitors.

Meanwhile in the March of 1993 the Secretary of State for Wales had presented a White Paper to Parliament entitled "A Charter for the Future" which was to have a direct effect on Llanelly. The proposal was to entail the merger of some of the Welsh councils and reduce their number to create all purpose Unitary Authorities. Within the scheme Llanelly Borough Council could either be a Unitary Authority in its own right or merge with Carmarthen and Dinefwr to form a new Carmarthenshire County Council. For Llanelly obviously the former was the preferred option, and there followed an intense period of lobbying for this in the halls of power, this was to be of no avail as the Local Government (Wales) Bill slowly passed through the various stages in Parliament and emerged with constitution of the Carmarthenshire County Council giving Llanelly just 33 seats on the new Authority.

Elections for the thirty three members to represent Llanelly and districts took place in May 1995; obscuring almost the honour accorded the Lord Lieutenant of Dyfed in the Queens New Year Honours. Sir David Mansel Lewis of Stradey Castle became a Knight Commander of the Victorian Order and awarded the C.B.E.

The private housing developments started in 1994 in the Machynys/Seaside area were now taking shape, and the leisure complex under the new management of Civic Leisure formulated a centre which included the refurbished Jubilee Swimming Pool with a Technogym, Badminton Courts, indoor cricket training centre, restaurant, function rooms and full time creche. The Prince of Wales was once again a visitor to Llanelly to reaffirm his links with the towns' business, industrial and civic leaders and youth.

With the impending handing over of the authority to the new Carmarthenshire Authority Llanelly was to witness the sad event of the laying down of the Colours of the 4th Battalion Royal Regiment of Wales at the Parish Church. Trooping of the Colours from the Drill Hall to take the final salute in front of the Town Hall was watched by the inhabitants prior to the final event.

Demolition work in the old market precinct through to Murray Street was completed to make way for the towns' new shopping centre, as the new coastal link road was officially opened. Another boost to the centre was the announcement by ASDA that it was their intention to participate in the market development and establish their superstore in Llanelly's new shopping complex.

Early in 1996 alongside the already established C.F.Taylor aircraft furnishing manufacturing plant Sillock Duval established their plastic moulding facility at the Dafen Industrial Park, which with Avon Inflatables and Daniel Fans factories made it a thriving centre.

April 1996 saw the final nail in the coffin of the Llanelly Borough Council which ceased to exist under the changeover to the Carmarthenshire County Council and the end of another era in the history of the town. The huge efforts of the Borough Council had given a massive impetus to their development schemes which were now to come to fruition with the Coastal Park Scheme emerging as a total entity. The town had been well served by the local representatives and authorities in the Borough who can be proud of their achievements in their services to the town.

1998 saw the final curtain on the oldest brewery in the town. Following its merger with Crown in 1988, the Brewery had continued to make beers under the Crown Buckley leadership, unfortunately a national trend in the drinking habits of the UK generally saw the sale of beer radically reduce. The younger element had changed to drinking lager and wine, and the strict laws of "drinking and driving" were to leave an indelible mark on public house drinking. The Brewery closed down with only an empty shell of an old building as its monument.

The same limitations affected the style of the pubs, and many were revamped as "theme pubs" for the young or family eating places, thereby ending the primary purpose of the public house as a social meeting place.

The prominence of the National Eisteddfod to Wales and the Welsh people is important not only for its cultural significance but also for the revenue which it brings to the host town. As a consequence the location and planning is critical to make the whole event a success. With the event in Llanelly in the year 2000 this meant that as the site was an integral part of the Millenium Project all things relevant to the event had to be completed to an exacting schedule. The Millenium Coastal Project was dependent upon the combined assistance and sponsorship of the Millenium Commission, Carmarthenshire County Council, Welsh Development Agency, European Development Funding Council, Welsh Assembly, Forestry Authority, C.A.D.W. and the Welsh Water Authority, in all relationships and co-operation were critical.

The £27.5 million pound scheme is designed to enhance and preserve the natural environment and wildlife habitant of a stretch of coastline from Lougher to Pembrey where it would link with the already established Country Park. Along this length it was to feature diverse attractions each linked to the next by a continuous cycle and footpath of 22 kilometres from end to end.

At the eastern end an addition to the Wildfowl Centre would include a new wetland habitant, Black Poplar woodland and fishing lakes. The Machynys peninsular was to accommodate an 18 hole golf course, holiday village, coarse fishing lake, salt marsh, bird hide and observation point. A "Park and Ride" carpark was also to be sited from which a land train would link the area to the Millenium Park Centre at the North Dock.

The already well established Centre at the North Dock overlooking the beach and seafront walk will eventually have a cycle hire facility. A short distance from the Centre are the Eisteddfod Fields and Sandy Water Park which can be reached by a walkway along the coast or a short drive along the coastal link road. Features at the Eisteddfod Fields include a lookout point at high level giving uninterrupted views across the estuary, a new Gorsedd Circle of standing stones, and walkways around the water park with grassed areas and carparking facility. In addition the area can be reached from the town by a new walkway and bridge over the coastal link road.

The old North Dock has been transformed after major dredging to remove sand and silt and the basin relined. This together with the addition of a sluice cell to maintain the level of water provides a perfect marina for all types of aquatic events. It is hoped that the future will see a wide variety of watersports and exhibitions at the site on a regular basis for many years to come.

Between the Eisteddfod Fields and Burry Port harbour is a proposed "Greenway Corridor" through which the cycle path with its earth sculpture, rest and picnic sites will pass. The foreshore area will be given up to a campsite and urban park area, with wildlife habitats and trails across open areas.

At Burry Port, the harbour will be refurbished to give a marina style working harbour, with visitor facilities such as a café, cycle hire depot and tourist information desk. Improved parking facilities for public access and viewing will be enhanced by repaved dockside surrounds and landscaped parkland.

The Coastal Park meets up with the already well established Pembrey Country Park and beaches at its western end. In all a magnificent project against which there is no other comparable scheme in the country.

The project has already fulfilled one of the objectives of its concept, that of providing the impressive site for the National Eisteddfod of Wales for the year 2000. To understand the significance of this event to the people of Wales one has to go back to medieval times of a thousand years ago when large areas of Wales and the Marches were governed by independent Kings and Princes.

Each court had its own poet who was accorded his seat or chair in the household of its lord. Today the modern Eisteddfod awards a ceremonial chair to the winner of a composition annually of a 200 line poem, after presentation of the award he or she keeps.

In the eighteenth century and early part of the nineteenth century the majority of Wales in more populated areas was owned by the landed gentry who were either of English extraction or had become anglicised Welsh who through their wealth had drawn away from the lower classes. As a consequence the Welsh language and culture suffered from lack of support and patronage.

The Gorsedd of Bards was an association of individuals dedicated to the preservation of the Welsh language, literature, music and culture. Its membership is by invitation, and on entry to the circle each new member adopts a bardic title. The stature within the Gorsedd order of each member can be distinguished by the colour of their robes, either white, blue or green and worn at all ceremonies. The members elect from among their group a leader, then given the title Archdruid, and who then chairs the Eisteddfod and leads the presentation of the awards. Other officers for the Eisteddfod are elected from the ranks of the group in keeping with the ceremonies, the Keeper of the Grand Sword, Presenter of the Hirlas Horn and Presenter of the Flower Token all have their place in the order.

One year before the Eisteddfod the Archdruid attended by the Gorsedd of Bards will meet on a specially laid out circle of stones at the venue selected for the next pending Eisteddfod to publicly proclaim the event. The main ceremonies of the Eisteddfod which take place at the end of the event are the awards for the winners of entries of a specific nature, a crown to the author of the best verse in non-traditional metre, a literature medal for a work of prose and, the most coveted prize, that of a chair for the composition of a 200 line poem in strict traditional metre.

Each Eisteddfod is supervised by the National Eisteddfod Council and its permanent Director who liase with the committees of local volunteers who draw up the programme of events and organise fund raising and support from local trade, industry and municipal authorities. The modern Eisteddfod which has developed since around 1900 is a cultural festival attended by more than 200,000 visitors and participants from all over the world, and although Welsh is the only language used on stage in the main pavilions, there is provision for translation facilities over the eight days of events held at the beginning of August each year.

Llanelly has hosted the Eisteddfod on six occasions including that of the millennium year, namely:-

1856: This the earliest recorded was a one day event held in the rear gardens of Llanelly House.

1895: The first of an eight day event in Llanelly in which the main ceremonies in the modern format took place in the market hall.

1903: Proclamation took place at the Logan Stone in Peoples Park and the Eisteddfod followed from the same site.

1930: The site was again Peoples Park.

1962: Proclaimed at the Gorsedd Circle in Park Howard at the Eisteddfod at Penygaer Fields, although there was community singing, Noson Lawen style in the gardens in front of the Town Hall which went on until 2am in the morning at the end of the festivities.

2000: At the most impressive site ever for the event on the specially designed Millennium Coastal Park complex which included a new Gorsedd Circle, a main pavilion with seating for 4,000 visitors, many satellite marquees for lesser events, craft exhibitions, literature, arts and lecture theatre. Away from the western end is a series of camping sites for participants and visitors.

This then is the Llanelly in the year 2000A.D., with still some links with a changed industrial base. British Steel's Trostre Works, Ina Needle Bearings, Calasonic's Llanelly Radiators Ltd., Huntsman (Chemicals) UK Ltd., Avon Inflatable Products, 3K's Heavy Engineering, Daniel Fans, Delta Enfield Cables and Dyfed Steel (Stockholders) Ltd.

The trend now is irreversible as Llanelly looks to the future for its survival in the success of its bid for the top as the tourism centre for Wales.

Significant Buildings

Adulam Baptist Chapel Felinfoel (rebuilt 1840) 1709
Wind Street Wesleyan Chapel (rebuilt 1793) 1780
Capel Als (enlarged 1831) 1780
Horeb Chapel (Five Roads) 1832
Nos. 17-19 Goring Road (houses) 1836c
Park Street Independent Chapel 1839
Capel Newydd(cm) rebuilt; Bethel (Seaside); Siloah (Seaside) 1840
Westfa House (Felinfoel) 1845
Railway Goods Station 1852
Stradey Castle; Wesleyan Church (Hall Street); 1855
Athenaeum (Public Library) – Porch destroyed 1926 1857
St. Pauls (Ann Street) 1857
Greenfield (Baptist) Murray Street 1858
Zion Chapel (Baptist) Upper Park Street 1858
Trinity (CM); Holy Trinity (Felinfoel) 1858
Athenaeum Tower & Neville Gallery added 1864
Park Congregational Church 1864
Ael-Y-Bryn House (Felinfoel) 1865
Highfield House (Caswell Street) 1865
Park Church (Murray Street) 1865
Capel y Doc (Independent) New Dock Road 1867
Bethania (Baptist) 1869
St Peters Church (Paddock Street) 1869
Houses; Stepney Street & Vaughan Street 1870
Hall Street Church (Wesleyan); Moriah (Baptist) 1870
All Saints Vicarage (rear Goring Rd/Old Rd) 1871
Presbyterian Church (Stepney Street) 1873
Stradey Castle (tower added) 1874
Barclays Bank (Vaughan Street) 1875
Siloah (CM) 1876
Ebeneezer Chapel (Independent) 1881
Bryncaerau Castle (Mansion House, Park Howard) 1885
Llanelly Hospital (Marble Hall Road) 1885
All Saints-extended; Christ Church (Morfa) 1887
Calfaria (Baptist) Ann Street 1887
Parish Hall; Market Hall 1887
Houses; Old Road, New Road, Felinfoel Road   1890
Nos. 22-24 Cowell Street 1890
Mansell Arms; Lucania Building 1890
Coleshill School 1891
Castle Chambers (corner of Murray Street) 1893
Caersalem (Baptist) Marsh Street 1893
Town Hall (Spring Gardens); Stepney Arcade 1894
Market Pavilion 1895
Soar (Independent) Marsh Street 1896
North Dock 1897-1902

Melbourne Hotel (Station Road) 1900
Park Church restoration 1905-1907
Glenalla (CM) Chapel 1909
Capel Newydd (façade reconstructed) 1910
Lloyds Bank (Stepney Street) 1910
Lychgate of Parish Church rebuilt 1911
Midland Bank (John Street) 1912
St Albans Church 1912
Exchange Buildings 1915

(1) "The Dell" House in Furnace was built by Alexander Raby between 1796 and 1800, no exact date given.
(2) "Penyfai House", there is a dispute over the date of this building but would appear to be between 1830 and 1860. Burned down and rebuilt in 1924.
(3)
(1)

HOTELS and PUBLIC HOUSES of LLANELLI in 1897

Half Moon Inn	1 Als Square
Oddfellows Arms	59 Upper Ann Street
Beaufort Arms	Lower Ann Street
Bull Inn	80 Lower Ann Street
Prince of Wales	86 Lower Ann Street
Mermaid Inn	1 Biddulph Street
King's Head	17 Bridge Street
Bryn Terrace Hotel	6 Bryn Terrace
Britannia Hotel	9 Bryn Terrace
Lord Nelson Inn	Bryn Road
Sea View Inn	15 Bwlch y Gwynt
Cornish Arms	Cambrian Street
Salutation Hotel	Church Street
British Tar	Church Street
Union Inn	Church Street
Ship Inn	3 Upper Church Street
Three Crowns	6 Upper Church Street
Marquis of Granby Inn	Dafen Row
Duke of Wellington	65 Dillwyn Street
Dimpath Inn	Dimpath Terrace
Smiths Arms	Dolau Road
Dock Hotel	Embankment Road
Trevose Inn	17 Glanmor Road
Globe Inn	Globe Row, Dafen
Old Red Cow	Hall Street
George & Dragon	Hall Street
Castle Inn	14 Hall Street
Union Hall	10 Hall Street
Black Horse	8 Hall Street
Prince of Wales	6 Hall Street
Cornish Arms	King's Square
Royal Park	King's Square
Glanmor Inn	1 Marine Street
Cardigan Arms	7 Marine Street
Trafalgar Inn	11 Marine Street
Albion Inn	8 Marine Street
Sailors Home	Marine Street
Stepney Arms	7 Market Street
Greyhound Hotel	11 Market Street
Barley Mow Inn	13 Market Street
Bush Inn	29 Market Street
Royal Exchange	Market Street
Dynevor Castle	18 Market Street
Black Lion	16 Market Street
Bird in Hand	12 Market Street

Golden Lion	2 Market Street
Albion Hotel	5 Murray Street
Malabar Hotel	7 Murray Street
Cricketer's Arms	Murray Street
Raven Inn	Murray Street
Clarence Hotel	Murray Street
Bres Arms	Murray Street
Queen Victoria	Murray Street
Northumberland Hotel	New Dock Street
Steam Packet Inn	New Dock Street
Bird in Hand Inn	New Dock Street
Marine Hotel	New Dock Street
Harbour View Hotel	New Dock Street
Rose & Crown	New Dock Road
Whitstable Inn	New Dock Road
Neptune Inn	New Dock Road
Three Mariners	New Dock Road
Penrhos Inn	New Dock Road
New Inn	New Dock Road
Biddulph Inn	19 New Street
Old Castle Inn	Old Castle Road
Ty Melyn Hotel	10 Park Street
Stepney Arms Hotel	Park Street
Bristol Tavern	13 Park Street
Ivy Bush Inn	5 Park Street
Swansea Castle	Upper Park Street
Stag's Head Inn	Pembrey Road
New Market House	29 Prospect Place
Welsh Star	1 Railway Terrace
Whitehall Inn	Station Road
Waterloo Inn	Station Road
Rolling Mill	Station Road
Vine Inn	24 Station Road
Pemberton Arms	32 Station Road
Railway Station Hotel	44 Station Road
Railway Hotel	83 Station Road
Oddfellows Inn	85 Station Road
Melbourne Hotel	79 Station Road
Foresters Arms	77 Station Road
Apple Tree Inn	75 Station Road
North Gate Hotel	28 Stepney Street
Centre Hotel	24 Stepney Street
Cambrian Hotel	2 Stepney Street
Brecon Arms	29 Swan Street
Star Hotel	117 Swansea Road
Boars Head	28 Swansea Road
Lamb & Flag	21 Swansea Road

Crown & Anchor	31 Thomas Street
Farmers Arms Hotel	37 Thomas Street
Thomas Arms Hotel	Thomas Street
Fountain Inn	36 Thomas Street
Drover's Arms	30 Thomas Street
Mason's Arms	24 Thomas Street
Rose & Crown	Thomas Street
Anchor Inn	2 Tinwork Row, Morfa
Vale of Neath	2 Tunnel Road
Bisley Arms	10 Union Square
Hope & Anchor	Victoria Road
Greenfield Inn	Victoria Road
Angel Inn	Water Street
Swan & Theatre Vaults	Water Street
White Hart Hotel	23 Water Street
Stevenson's Bottling Stores	27 Water Street
Square & Compass	29 Water Street
Princess Head	West End
Saddlers Arms	14 Wind Street
Union Inn	Victoria Road
Sloop Aground	Dolau Road
West End Inn	West End
Ship & Pilot Inn	9 Marine Street
Friends Inn	15 Marine Street
Cambrian Hotel	35 Marine Street
Globe Hotel	Maliphant Row
Rose & Crown	Paddock Street
Dillwyn Arms	Dillwyn Street

LLANELLY SCHOOLS

Schools in the area were initially subscribed to by the churches and as a consequence under the supervision of their minister. One of the earliest recorded of these was the Parish Church School under Vicar James Penaud who in 1741 held a register of 44 scholars.

The first regular school for boys and girls was started by Vicar Morris at the Wern, in which classes were also held in the Parish Church. This was followed in 1865 by the "PenTip" National School under the direction of Rev. A.J.M.Green.

Between these dates, in 1840 the Hoel Fawr Schools were opened, and in 1844 four other schools were recorded:-

Rev. David Evans School	Church Street
Francis Francis School	Swansea Road
William Marks School	Prospect Place
William Williams School	Oxen Street

Other small establishments followed listing a total of fourteen by 1847 recorded by the Blue Book Register. In 1848 the Llanelly School opened, but there is no record of its exact location according to John Innes.

Marsh Street & Felinfoel Schools 1848

Dafen School 1850

Pen Tip School 1865

New Dock School 1867

Five Roads School 1868

Llwynhendy & Roman Catholic Schools 1870

Schools Board established 1871

Old Road Junior, Pontyates, Spitty, Felinfoel(Union Row),Wern Schools 1875

St Pauls Memorial School, Machynys School 1877

Church school(Llwynhendy) & Pemberton School(Lakefield) 1882

Old Road Infants School 1885

Prospect Place Infants School & Lakefield Infants School 1886

Furnace Schoolrooms (Infants) & Christchurch Infants (Morfa) 1889

Coleshill School 1891

Intermediate School (Marble Hall Road) 1897

Dafen, Ysgol Hebron (Globe Row, Dafen), Park Street, Capel School (Morfa) and Pembrey School 1900.

Llanelly House

Prior to the building of the old Llanelli House in 1714 by Sir Thomas Stepney 5th Baronet, an earlier building stood on the site thought to be as early as the late 16th/early 17th century, and the foundations of part of this has been presented in the current renovation programme via a small viewing section.

The original building for Sir Thomas Stepney, 5th Baronet was completed in 1714 and this is borne out by the date etched on the surviving leaden hopper head of heraldic design which still exists today. The house originally had been inherited by Margaret Vaughan, Sir Thomas's wife in 1706/1707. He remodelled the building, adding a third floor and hipped roof.

Sir John's eldest son Thomas (1725-1772) married Elenor Lloyd and lived at Llangennech Park until he became the 7th Baronet when he moved to Llanelli House.

Sir John Stepney, 8th Baronet (1743-1811) spent only his childhood at Llanelli House; as a diplomat he spent most of his time abroad.

He quarrelled with his brother Thomas and disinherited him, in his will he transferred the Llanelli estate to a series of friends, which finally came down to William Chambers. When Chambers died in 1855, and following a lengthy court case, the house was given back to the Stepney family.

During the period following William Chambers' death his son William Chambers Jnr (1809-1882) lived at the house and he was the founder of Llanelli Pottery in 1839. In the 1830's some renovation work to the second floor level was carried out by William Chambers.

Somewhere in the 19th century, when Llanelli House was tenanted and the ground floor converted into shops and offices, prior to which when the two retail units were introduced into the layout of the ground floor the main staircase was removed. It was suggested that these were used in the refurbishment of the Stepney Hotel (previously the "Ship and Castle" in Park Street). Sadly the hotel was demolished some years ago and the stairway was lost. Current work, however, includes a staircase modelled exactly on the original, and has been positioned in its old location in the house.

Following the passage of ownership through two more heirs, the house became the property of Lady Margaret Stepney, the widow of Sir Arthur Cowell Stepney, who with her daughter Catherine Meriel, began a refurbishment of two upper floors and installed a Georgian style staircase centrally from the hall. Thereafter, the house was used as a venue for local societies and voluntary organisations. Catherine married Sir Arthur Stafford Howard on the 18th September 1911, and this was the last prominent family event at the house. On receiving Borough status on 6 November 1913 the town elected Sir Stafford as the Charter Mayor for 1913/1914.

The house is now in the hands of the Carmarthenshire Heritage Trust, who are responsible for returning the house to its original state. Having recently visited Llanelli House on a tour to see the work already done, I would recommend a visit to see for yourself the incredible standard of workmanship that they have achieved in every detail of the work, and the house is now home to some of the original art and artefacts.

Back of Llanelly House in 1863

Part of Llanelly House 1902

Llanelly House 2014

The Stables at Llanelly House

Bryn Jones of
Bryn Terrace, Seaside,
Llanelli

Etta Daniels
Old Castle Public House, Old Castle Road, Llanelli
Later married Mr. Geoff Longhurst and moved to Swiss Valley

Shown are (from Left)
Cliff and Kathy Evans, Bryn Jones, I. Randall
Mr and Mrs Evans lived at the Cardigan Dairy on Dolau Road, Llanelli, and
who owned the stables and riding school until 1914 when he enlisted

Llanelly House Restoration
May 2014

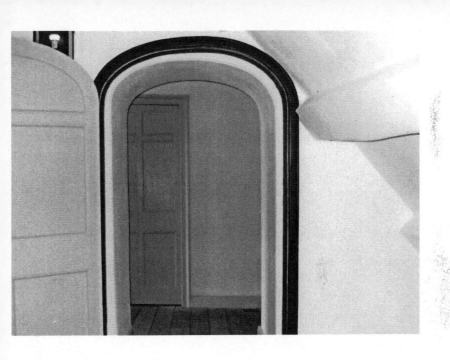

References

Old Llanelly ....John Jones 1901

Coal Mining Llanelly to 1850...................................Malcolm V Symonds 1982

Llanelly Pottery...Gareth Hughs / Robert Pugh

The Workers ....Tony Evans

The Pub and the Pulpit..Llanelli Library

The Chartered Borough of Llanelly............................Llanelli Borough Council

The National Eisteddfod 2000 ....Eisteddfod Council

Felinfoel Brewery ....Promotional - Felinfoel Brewery

Tinopolis ....John Edwards

Looking Around Llanelly.................................. Harry Davies / Gareth Hughes

Llanelly Chronicles...Gareth Hughes

Llanelly Landscapes.. David Q Bowen

Llanelly Lives ....H M Jones

Llanelli Library Archives

Remembrance of a Riot 1911..John Edwards

A History of the Llanelly Borough Council.............................David F Griffiths